. . . .

MANAGING A SMOOTH TRANSITION
FROM AID DEPENDENCE
IN AFRICA

POLICY ESSAY NO. 28

MANAGING A SMOOTH TRANSITION

FROM AID DEPENDENCE

IN AFRICA

Carol Lancaster and
Samuel Wangwe

Distributed by the
Johns Hopkins University Press

Published Jointly by the
Overseas Development Council and the
African Economic Research Consortium
Washington, DC

Copyright © 2000 by Overseas Development Council, Washington, DC

Distributed by:
The Johns Hopkins University Press
2715 North Charles Street
Baltimore, MD 21218-4319
web site: www.press.jhu.edu/press/index.htm

Library of Congress Cataloging-In-Publication Data

Lancaster, Carol
   Managing a Smooth Transition from Aid Dependence in Africa / Carol Lancaster and Samuel Wangwe
      p. cm. — (Policy essay; no. 28)
      Includes bibliographical references.
      ISBN 1-56517-032-6
      1. Economic assistance—Africa, Sub-Saharan. 2. Africa, Sub-Saharan—Economic conditions—1960- 3. Africa, Sub-Saharan—Economic policy. I. Wangwe, S. M. II. Title. III. Series.

HC800 .L358 2000
338.967—dc21

          00-050123

Printed in the United States of America.

Editor: Jacqueline Edlund-Braun
Cover design: Design Consultants, Inc.

OVERSEAS DEVELOPMENT COUNCIL ·

Contents

Foreword

Two major trends in African development are coming together. The first is the now widespread understanding that Sub-Saharan Africa is the major development challenge of the next decade. The second is the growing belief that development aid, while achieving some success in Africa, must be changed considerably if it is to be more effective in promoting Africa's development in a manner less intrusive and directive. Ironically, the practices of development agencies in the past have contributed, albeit inadvertently, to Africa's problems. At the same time, however, aid programs also can be part of the answer to Africa's problems—but only if the lessons of the past are reflected in changed policies. This Policy Essay, *Managing a Smooth Transition from Aid Dependence in Africa*, is designed to that end.

In this, ODC's twenty-eighth Policy Essay, Carol Lancaster and Samuel Wangwe examine the nature, extent, and impact of aid dependence and address the critical challenge of how to lessen the dependence of most African governments on bilateral and multilateral aid, while accelerating the continent's economic and social progress. The essay is designed to provide decision makers, particularly in bilateral and multilateral development agencies, with concrete policy recommendations on how to promote the development choices of Africans in a way that lessens the dependency of African policies on continued flows of concessional resources from external sources.

This Policy Essay is a key component of a larger project conducted by the African Economic Research Consortium (AERC) in collaboration with the Overseas Development Council (ODC). In carrying out the larger project, joint teams of analysts from Africa and donor countries produced a set of framework papers that explored the concept of aid dependence and its extent, and a set of country case studies. The Policy Essay presented here is a natural extension of this earlier project work.

We are fortunate to have attracted two outstanding directors to lead the project and co-author this essay. Carol Lancaster is a Visiting Fellow at

ODC and a Professor at Georgetown University's School of Foreign Service. Samuel Wangwe is Director of the Economic and Social Research Foundation in Dar es Salaam, Tanzania. We are grateful for their leadership. We are also appreciative of the dedication of the project's steering committee for their expertise and guidance throughout the project.

This project continues the ongoing and fruitful collaboration between the AERC and ODC. That relationship began in 1996 with a major study of how to revive growth in Africa: *Agenda for Africa's Economic Renewal*, edited by Benno Ndulu and Nicolas van de Walle (Transaction Publishers, 1996). This evolved into a subsequent ODC study of how to improve the performance of the major aid donors to Africa, which culminated in a Policy Essay entitled *Improving Aid to Africa*, by Nicolas van de Walle and Timothy Johnston (ODC, 1996). Along with a broad dissemination to English audiences, this essay was also published and distributed in French (*Repenser l'aide à l'Afrique*, Karthala, 1999).

We are grateful to the Swedish International Development Cooperation Agency, the U.S. Agency for International Development, the Department for International Development of the United Kingdom, the Swiss Agency for Development and Cooperation, and the Government of Japan that have provided financial support for this project. In addition, ODC's participation in the project has been made possible by the long-standing and generous support from the Ford Foundation for the Council's overall activities.

John W. Sewell
President
Overseas Development Council

Delphin G. Rwegasira
Executive Director
African Economic Research
Consortium

October 2000

Acknowledgments

In any large research project such as this, there are many individuals who contribute in important ways to the project's activities, findings, and conclusions. We greatly appreciate all their contributions, named or unnamed. At the same time, we acknowledge that all errors and omissions are our own.

We are grateful to the project's steering committee and the committee's co-chairs, Catherine Gwin (ODC) and Augustin Fosu and Ibrahim Elbadawi (AERC), for advising on the substantive elements of the project. In addition to the project coordinators and a representative from each of the collaborating institutions, the steering committee included experts from the research and policy communities in African and donor countries. (For a full listing of the steering committee members, please see p. 70 in this volume.)

Ali Ali, Ky Amoako, Deborah Brautigam, Dag Ehrenpreis, Alan Gelb, John W. Sewell, and Kazuo Takahashi provided encouragement and constructive comments on the draft manuscript. Deena LaMarque, Helen Lawuo, and Darlene Mutalemwa provided valuable research assistance. Particular thanks are also due to Kathryn Imboden for her help in organizing a major conference in Berne on this issue.

And finally, we would like to thank our funders for making the project and this essay possible: the Swedish International Development Cooperation Agency, the U.S. Agency for International Development, the Department for International Development of the United Kingdom, the Swiss Agency for Development and Cooperation, and the Government of Japan.

Introduction

Most of the 48 countries of Sub-Saharan Africa[1] are among the poorest in the world, with the largest proportions of their populations in poverty, the lowest indicators of social progress, and, for many years, the slowest rates of growth. Most have also depended on foreign aid to fund significant amounts of their investment and consumption. Is there a connection between the relatively high levels of aid dependence in Africa and the poor economic performance of most of the region? In short, could aid dependence[2] be one of the problems of development in Africa rather than one of the solutions? This question—not a new one in the discourse on aid and development—has been raised again in recent years as experts seek explanations for Africa's disappointing development record. This policy essay addresses this question.

This volume is part of a collaborative research project to assess the nature and extent of the problem of aid dependence in Africa, deepen the understanding of its impact, and provide suggestions on how to bring about a smooth reduction of aid dependence so as to enhance rather than disrupt development in the region and promote appropriate integration of Africa into the world economy.

There is a large and diverse literature on the causes of Africa's disappointing development experience. These causes include geography—the consequences of being in the tropics and the existence of many small, landlocked countries. They include the burden of colonial history and the long-term consequences of the slave trade that robbed many communities of their most productive members. They include the impact of the international economy, which over the past several decades has been volatile and unfriendly to exporters of many primary products (which includes nearly all African countries). Nevertheless, over the past two decades a degree of consensus has evolved among development specialists that declining terms of trade, faulty policies, and weak institutions have been at the heart of the African development problem.

In the past decade, the discourse on development in Africa has also begun to focus on the effectiveness of foreign aid in promoting African development. Aid flows to the region have been large relative to the size of most African economies. Yet rates of growth have remained low. A number of recent econometric studies of aid and growth worldwide come to different conclusions regarding the relationship between them. Most of these studies show that aid has a positive but usually small impact on growth *if* macroeconomic and other conditions are favorable.[3] Such a result may not be surprising in many parts of the world where aid flows have been small relative to the size of recipient economies. But in Africa, where aid has been relatively large, this is an unexpected result. And while evaluations of aid effectiveness by multiple aid donors confirm that aid in Africa has had some outstanding successes, overall aid in Africa has also been among the least effective and least sustainable in the world.[4]

We know that part of the explanation for the relative ineffectiveness of aid in Africa relates to the difficult and challenging physical and economic environments common throughout the region. Poor policy and institutional environments in which the aid has been provided are also an important explanation in many countries. Aid cannot be effective where the incentives for investment, production, and growth are lacking because prices are distorted, taxes are excessive, corruption is rampant, and property is insecure.

It has also been increasingly recognized in recent years that added to the impediments to development and effective aid in African countries are those unintentionally created by the donors of that aid. Donor governments and international organizations have often provided aid for bureaucratic, political, and commercial objectives that have overridden (and at times, undercut) development concerns, leading to ineffective aid from a developmental standpoint. In addition, many donors have found it difficult to change their conventional practices and procedures even if such change is perceived to be consistent with enhancing aid effectiveness.

More recently, attention has begun to focus on the question of whether the very size of aid flows themselves and the dependence of African countries on the aid, together with the way the aid is managed by donors, have contributed to the poor development performance in the region.

We know that under the right circumstances, foreign aid can boost development by funding the expansion of crucial investments (for example, in education, health, or infrastructure); provide needed technical assistance and training for government officials and others; finance research that can increase the productivity of resources; and encourage needed reforms. It can even fund expanded consumption, which—again, under the right circumstances—can foster economic progress. How, then, might large flows of aid over an extended period discourage development?

Foreign aid, when it is large and continuous, can have unintended, negative impacts in recipient countries. For example, it can appreciate the exchange rate (and so, discourage exports) and ratchet up the government budget. Relatively large amounts of aid can also have an impact on the incentives that affect the behavior of political and economic agents—potentially reducing the accountability of government leaders to their own peoples and the willingness of officials to tackle difficult economic and political reforms. The way the aid is managed, both by recipient governments and donor aid agencies, can also have an impact on the functioning of the government bene- fiting from it. Where large amounts of aid are poorly managed—for example, where the aid is not provided to fund a coherent set of priority activities, where it creates unfunded future budgetary commitments, and where it is not integrated into development plans of the recipient government—it may not only be wasted but can undercut planning and budgetary discipline on the part of the government and so weaken public institutions. And where the aid flows are large (and provided by multiple donor agencies), these poten- tially negative consequences can be significant and broad reaching.

This study finds that aid dependence in Africa can be beneficial from a development perspective and has not per se been a cause of the poor devel- opment performance. Botswana, a country heavily dependent on foreign aid, has had one of the most successful development performances of any country in the world. Foreign aid appears to have been quite effective in Botswana and contributed to its rapid economic and social progress. (Botswana was also blessed with rich mineral deposits that the government has managed well.)

In a number of other countries in Africa, however, aid dependence appears to have contributed to poor economic performance. But it has not only been the size of aid flows that has played this role, but also the way the large flows have been handled by both donors and recipients. Large amounts of aid over an extended period from multiple and uncoordinated donors pro- vided to weak and often poorly coordinated government ministries have further weakened those ministries and undercut key government processes (especially planning and budgeting). As a result, the aid has likely contri- buted to poor development performance in aid dependent countries in Africa. In short, aid dependence, can make the strong stronger and the weak weaker.

. . . .

THE PLAN OF THE STUDY

■   THIS BOOK IS BASED ON A TWO-YEAR COLLABORATIVE research project under the auspices of the Overseas Development Council (ODC) and the

African Economic Research Consortium (AERC), entitled "Managing a Smooth Transition from Aid Dependence in Africa." This project was supported by the Swedish International Development Agency, the U.S. Agency for International Development, the Department for International Development of the United Kingdom, the Swiss Agency for Development and Cooperation, and the Government of Japan. It has sought to:

- define aid dependence;

- assess the characteristics and consequences of that dependence for African economies and institutions; and

- identify strategies for reducing dependence on foreign aid in countries of Sub-Saharan Africa.

The study was carried out by joint teams of scholars from Africa and from donor countries. It commissioned a set of eight framework papers on the dimensions of aid dependence and approaches for reducing it.[5] These papers also provided guidance to the second component of the project that consisted of eight case studies covering a cross section of countries by region, language, size, resource endowment, and level of development: Botswana, Burkina Faso, Ethiopia, Mali, Mozambique, Tanzania, Uganda, and Zambia.[6] The case studies aimed to show the nature and extent of aid dependence, its impact, and strategies for managing and reducing it in specific country contexts, applying the findings of the framework papers to specific countries. The material in this volume is a synthesis of these 16 papers, combined with the analytical and policy perspectives of the authors of this essay. It is expected that the framework papers and case studies will be published by the AERC in two companion volumes—one of the framework papers, the other of the case studies.

This essay addresses four key questions related to a smooth transition from aid dependence in Africa:

- What is aid dependence?

- What are the causes and consequences of aid dependence?

- What has been the experience of particular countries with aid dependence?

- What are the most important elements for aid donors and recipients to consider in a strategy to reduce aid dependence?

Chapter One examines the meaning of aid dependence. Chapter Two assesses its effects in Africa. And, finally, Chapter Three offers strategies for managing a smooth transition from aid dependence in the future.

This study is built on the (still limited) body of research on aid dependence, much of it funded by the Swedish government. It attempts to advance the discourse by proposing a value-free definition of aid dependence, by exploring in detail the elements and impact of aid dependence in Africa, by proposing strategies for managing aid dependence and for decreasing it in the future.

This essay is intended to contribute not only to the ongoing discussion of how foreign aid can be reshaped to more effectively support development in Sub-Saharan Africa but also to the broader discourse on the challenges and opportunities of development in the region. Much is already known about the conditions in Africa that have slowed development there. It is less acknowledged that the aid interventions of foreign governments and international organizations pose unintended impediments to development in Africa. If Africa is to develop and if foreign aid is to make the kind of beneficial contribution it promises, both parties to the development challenge—the Africans *and* those governments and organizations wishing to help them—must reshape and reform their policies and the nature of their collaboration. This essay and the research project on which it is based are intended to help move this broad reform process forward.

NOTES

[1] This essay focuses only on countries of Sub-Saharan Africa, from which all of the case studies are drawn. "Africa" is thus used interchangeably with "Sub-Saharan Africa" throughout the essay, unless otherwise noted.

[2] Aid dependence is defined here as a situation of high aid intensity in which a government (or other entity) would suffer serious disruption if aid flows to it were terminated or significantly cut over a short period of time. This definition is further explained and elaborated in Chapter One of this volume.

[3] For a review of these studies and their findings see Development Assistance Committee, *Development Cooperation 1999 Report* (Paris: Organization for Economic Cooperation and Development, 2000), p.127, ff.

[4] For more on the effectiveness of aid to Africa from individual governments and international organizations, see Carol Lancaster, *Aid to Africa* (Chicago: University of Chicago Press, 1999); see also Nicolas van de Walle and Timothy Johnston, *Improving Aid to Africa*, Policy Essay No. 21 (Washington, DC: ODC, 1996).

[5] The framework papers for this project included:

1) Jean-Paul Azam and Seraphin Fouda, "The Economic Impact of Aid on Recipients"

2) Nicolas van de Walle, "Managing Aid to Africa: The Rise and Decline of the Structural Adjustment Regime"

3) Ravi Kanbur, "A Framework for Thinking Through Reduced Aid Dependence in Africa"

4) Stephen O'Connell and Charles Soludo, "Aid Intensity"

5) Kwesi Botchwey and Deborah Brautigam, "The Impact of Aid Dependence on Governmance and Institutions in Africa"

6) S. Devarajan, A.S. Rajkumar, and V. Swaroop, "What Does Aid to Africa Finance?"

7) Sam Wangwe and Carol Lancaster, "What is Aid Dependence?"

8) K. Y. Amoako and Ali Ali, "Financing Development in Africa: Some Exploratory Results"

[6] The case study authors and their respective study countries included:

1) Gervase Maipose and Gloria Somolekae (Botswana)

2) Savadogo Kimseyinga (Burkina Faso)

3) Befekadu Degefe and Kibre Moges (Ethiopia)

4) Dominique Njinkeu, Massaoly Coulibaly, and Abdramane Traore (Mali)

5) Robert Tibana and Pedro Couto (Mozambique)

6) Samuel Wangwe, Peter Noni, and Deo Mutalemwa (Tanzania)

7) Germina Ssemogerere and William Kalema (Uganda)

8) Oliver Saasa and Inyambo Mwanawina (Zambia)

Chapter 1
What Is
Aid Dependence?

"Aid dependence" is one of those itinerant terms, so common in social science discourse, that lacks a fixed or precise meaning.[1] It is used to refer to very different conditions and thus often blurs rather than clarifies communication. This chapter defines aid dependence for the purpose of this study and offers some measures of aid dependence in Africa and elsewhere. It also asks what aid actually finances in Africa, because how the aid is spent can affect the degree of dependence. It concludes by examining debt as an element in aid dependence.

. . . .

TOWARD A DEFINITION
OF AID DEPENDENCE

■   A REVIEW OF THE LIMITED LITERATURE on this subject suggests that there are, in fact, three main uses of the term "aid dependence." Many define it as simply a condition of large inflows of aid (i.e., official development assistance, or ODA) relative to key economic variables.[2] Another frequently used approach is to define aid dependence as "bad aid," that is, aid that is ineffective and results in a lessening of self-reliance on the part of the recipient or a surrender of control to the aid donor over recipient policies or other unwelcome conditions.[3] A third, rather different definition of aid dependence draws its inspiration from the "gap filling" approach on foreign aid and development.[4] It defines aid dependence as a situation in which the aid recipient needs the aid—in effect, depends on it—to achieve certain goals. These quite different definitions, all legitimate in their own right, illustrate the importance of defining aid dependence clearly at the outset.

Foreign aid provides resources to governments, private organizations, and individuals, much like other sources of resources such as taxation, foreign borrowing, private contributions, or earnings from wages, sales, or exports. Governments and others receiving significant amounts of aid over an extended period of time almost always spend that aid, adjusting their budgets, activities, employment, and often organizational size and structure to its continued availability. To the extent that the aid is spent for goods and services within the recipient country, it will have a further multiplier effect—increasing indirect economic reliance on the aid beyond those who immediately benefit from it. If the aid were to be cut suddenly and significantly or to disappear altogether, the economy would have to adjust to fewer resources and a lower rate of absorption. These adjustments could be painful, economically disruptive, and even politically destabilizing.

It is this condition of reliance on a particular source of resources that is the basis for our concept of aid dependence for the purposes of this study. *Aid dependence, defined here, is a situation in which a government (or other entity) receiving concessional external assistance would suffer serious economic and possibly political repercussions if that aid were significantly reduced or eliminated in a short period of time.*[5] There are several important elements in this definition:

- First, ODA is large relative to the size of the recipient's economy and other important economic phenomena.

- Second, continue relatively large aid flows over an extended period of time. Short-term surges in aid—for example, emergency relief over a period of one or two years—would not lead to aid dependence because their limited availability over time would typically prevent the kinds of adjustments in expenditures, programs, and organizational structures that create that dependence.

- Third, aid funds will be spent when they become available or very soon thereafter rather than saved by the government or organization receiving them. Were they not spent, then, by definition, the recipient would not come to depend on them.

The definition of aid dependence used here is intended to be value-neutral. It does not take sides on the debate on whether aid dependence is good or bad for development. Many have argued that large amounts of aid over an extended period of time can help lift poor countries out of poverty. In their framework paper for this study, "Financing Development in Africa: Some Exploratory Results," K.Y. Amoako and Ali Ali estimate that the amount of aid required to reduce poverty levels in Africa by half by 2015 (and ultimately, to reduce aid dependence) would total $200 billion between 1999 and 2010.[6] The aid dependence implied by these levels would be extraordinarily high in a number of countries.

Others have argued that large amounts of aid over long time periods almost always have negative consequences on recipients because of their impact on economic variables and behavioral incentives in recipient countries.[7] The disagreements about the developmental consequences, both positive and negative, of relatively large aid flows over time illustrate why the *concept* of dependence needs to be separated from the *consequences* of dependence. To do otherwise can lead to confusion and ultimately to poor policy choices.

· ·

MEASURING AID DEPENDENCE

■ HOW DO WE KNOW WHEN A COUNTRY OR GOVERNMENT has become aid dependent as defined in this study? The definition used here does not permit us to measure aid dependence except ex post facto, once the aid is withdrawn. We have, therefore, used "aid intensity" as an indicator of aid dependence. We have defined aid intensity as "the size of [aid] flows relative to the categories of economic activity they are designed to support."[8] These categories include gross national product (GNP), population, imports, investment, and government spending. In their framework paper for this project, Stephen O'Connell and Charles Soludo calculated aid intensity ratios for Africa and other developing regions and for most of the African countries included as case studies. They refined the measures of ODA and the estimates of economic variables in recipient countries, as shown in Table 1.

Aid intensity in Sub-Saharan Africa has long been the highest of any major developing region in every category of indicators and remains so today. In several of the African countries included in the table—Mozambique, Uganda, and Zambia—ODA exceeded gross investment, and in most countries ODA equaled a fifth or more of GNP. When aid intensity is measured relative to GNP or other benchmarks—as a proportion of imports, gross investment, government expenditures (with technical assistance only), and government wages—most African countries fall in the upper quartile of the aid intensity rankings.

Looking back several decades, Africa's median aid was already high by historical standards in the 1970s. It then doubled over the next two decades in response to a deepening balance-of-payments crisis and as part of large structural adjustment programs. Aid intensity continued to rise through the 1980s in response to policy reforms that many countries in Africa adopted. It began to drop in the 1990s with the overall decline in aid flows and

Region	Real ODA per capita (dollars)	Net ODA as % of GNP	Net ODA as % of Imports*	Net ODA as % of Investment*	Net ODA as % of Government Expenditures*	Technical Cooperation Government Wages
Latin America	24.30	1.66	1.70	4.16	3.19	12.62
South Asia	15.89	6.96	21.24	31.12	20.49	28.09
High Performing Asian Countries	4.10	0.22	0.23	0.57	1.70	5.68
Sub-Saharan Africa	51.59	13.41	28.38	71.37	49.70	37.25
Botswana	94.59	3.4	2.64	5.02	5.07	17.95
Ethiopia	72.00	23.00	37.00	53.29	43.20	n/a
Burkina Faso	n/a	17.65	46.24	53.94	n/a	n/a
Mali	47.07	19.30	37.75	58.61	n/a	n/a
Mozambique	53.21	97.53	75.61	135.03	n/a	n/a
Tanzania	44.80	23.06	66.30	78.10	140.16	n/a
Uganda	80.33	20.51	70.06	104.87	n/a	n/a
Zambia	41.84	32.89	48.80	218.43	123.54	135.21

Notes: All official development figures (ODA) are net of interest payments. O'Connell and Soludo also calculated aid as a percentage of GNP using a purchasing power parity approach to estimate GNP rather than estimating GNP based on official foreign exchange rates (which tends to inflate GNP data in developing countries). This approach produces much lower ratios of foreign aid as a percentage of GNP in Africa and elsewhere (about two-thirds lower). But the ratio of aid to GNP in Africa remains by far the highest in the world (double the ratios of other regions).

*Excluding technical assistance

Sources: Stephen O'Connell and Charles Soludo, "Aid Intensity in Africa," background paper prepared for ODC/AERC Project on Managing a Transition from Aid Dependence in Africa, November 1998, Table 4. The data in the table are drawn from the OECD and the World Bank. These data do not include private giving by NGOs or corporations, which, though still quite small relative to ODA, appears to be increasing in Africa and worldwide. Reliable data on this type of aid are not available. Aid from governments through NGOs is, however, captured in these statistics. Data on Ethiopia and Tanzania are drawn from the respective country case studies.

the shift in aid flows to transitional economies in Eastern Europe and the former Soviet Union.

Among the cases studied for this project, only Botswana substantially reduced its aid intensity during the 1980s and 1990s. Other cases in this project—Mozambique, Tanzania, Uganda, and Zambia—showed an opposite trend, shifting from low to high levels of aid intensity, while Burkina Faso and Mali had high and rising levels of aid intensity. The downward trend in aid flows to Africa—dropping from a high of $18 billion in 1994 (in 1997 U.S. dollars) to $13 billion in 1998—and an improved growth performance in much of the region have begun to reduce aid intensity there. The most recent data from the Development Assistance Committee (DAC) of the Organization for Economic Cooperation and Development (OECD) show that net ODA as a percentage of recipients' GNP has now begun to fall for all of the countries included as case studies in this project except Burkina Faso and Mali. Nevertheless, aid intensity ratios remain much higher in Africa than similar ratios in most of the rest of the world and remain high by historical standards.[9]

. . . .

FROM AID INTENSITY
TO AID DEPENDENCE

■   DATA ON AID INTENSITY ARE THE BEST INDICATORS of aid dependence (as defined here) available at present. The question arises whether different types of aid—project aid, budgetary and balance of payments support, and technical assistance—create different degrees of aid dependence. For example, a number of aid practitioners hypothesize that aid for project finance can be more dependence creating than aid for budget support. Where project finance leads to an overextension of the state and in particular where such finance creates future claims on government expenditures for which financing is not available, governments can become more dependent on aid to fund the continuation of those projects.[10] Another plausible hypothesis regarding the type of aid and dependence on that aid is that technical assistance may create less dependence than program or project aid. Technical assistance typically involves the expenditure of aid funds on expatriate advisors who are usually supposed to improve the capacity of local personnel and so eliminate the need for their services. How much can we say about the differential impact of the type of aid on dependence? First, we must ask what aid actually finances in Africa.

. . . .

WHAT DOES AID TO AFRICA FINANCE?

■ AID IN AFRICA IS USED TO FINANCE SEVERAL TYPES of activities: discrete investment projects; technical assistance (which is at times part of investment projects but frequently free-standing); budget support, often through funding associated with macroeconomic and sectoral reform programs; and debt relief, through the cancellation of debt.

The largest proportion of aid worldwide has long been provided for investment projects—for example, the construction of infrastructure, the expansion of social services, or the financing of research. Technical assistance was a significant proportion of aid to Africa in the early years after independence when the number of trained nationals was limited. After declining over several decades, it appears to have risen again in recent years, reaching one-quarter of aid to Africa at present. Also in the early years of African independence, a significant proportion of aid was provided as budget support to governments, like that of Botswana, which did not yet have revenue flows adequate to finance their expenditures. Budget support fell during the 1970s but began to increase again during the 1980s with the rise in structural and sectoral adjustment programs, which provided aid in support of economic policy reforms. Additionally, aid for debt relief has increased in recent years as donor governments and multilateral development banks have moved to reduce the exceptionally high debt burden of African countries through bilateral debt restructuring or outright cancellation and through the World Bank-led initiative for reducing the multilateral debts of Highly Indebted Poor Countries (HIPC), many of which are in Africa.

Data on ODA from the DAC show that in 1998 a total of $13.8 billion in net aid disbursements was provided the countries of Sub-Saharan Africa.[11] (This does not include debt forgiveness.) The DAC does not break out aid to Africa according to its use, but in a recent report, the World Bank also estimated that program aid in support of economic reforms for the 30 African countries participating in the Special Program of Assistance (SPA) averaged $2.5 billion per year between 1997 and 1998 or slightly under 10 percent of total gross ODA.[12] Thus, the profile of aid to Africa in 1998 shows that most aid was still provided as part of project financing or free-standing technical assistance. Debt forgiveness is estimated by the World Bank to have amounted to an additional $8.7 billion (including arrears) per year between 1997 and 1998 for SPA countries.[13] In the enhanced HIPC Initiative (1999), some $20 billion of debt relief (in net present value terms) will be delivered, but the initiative still needs to be fully funded.

The categories of project and program aid can be misleading, however, in terms of the real uses of the aid. Aid is "fungible"—that is, it can be used to fund activities that the recipient government intended to finance in the absence of the aid. When this is the case, aid in effect frees up government resources to be used elsewhere—for other investments, consumption, tax reductions, debt servicing, war, or other purposes. The fungibility of aid is not necessarily a bad thing from the point of view of a country's overall economic performance—its use can benefit that performance, for example, where governments use it to fund well-chosen investment priorities, imports, or recurrent costs that they would not otherwise be able to finance or even when they use it to reduce an excessive tax burden.

How fungible is aid to Africa? A study undertaken for this project by Shantayanan Devarajan, Andrew Rajkumar, and Vinaya Swaroop, using a panel database from 18 countries in Sub-Saharan Africa, revealed several interesting findings.[14] Foreign aid (not including technical assistance grants) boosted government expenditures by nearly the amount of the aid (90 percent), indicating that governments were not simply using the aid to replace taxes. However, about half of the aid was used to fund external debt service. The rest of aid was divided equally as between funding capital and current accounts (i.e., funding investments and ongoing expenditures) by governments.

Aid flows in particular sectors such as health, industry, and agriculture proved highly fungible. The authors observed that "there is no evidence . . . that aid to these sectors is increasing spending in the sectors for which it was intended."[15] Aid to energy, transport, and communications was partially fungible; it did lead to an increase in overall government spending in these sectors. Aid to education was the least fungible; it was almost entirely spent in that sector.

In specific country case studies, fungibility of aid is shown to exist. Econometric analyses of what aid finances and its economic impact in Zambia came to the conclusion that aid is highly fungible except for the agriculture, education, and transport sectors. In fact, one-quarter of the aid is found to finance recurrent spending. A high proportion of aid also appears to be associated with the servicing of international debts. In Mali it was found that fungibility of aid reduces government efforts to generate revenue, which in turn leads to deteriorating relationships with donors and development partners.

Studies on Tanzania concluded that the fungibility of aid is an important contributor to the growth of the economy as evidenced by the increase in fungibility in the latter part of the 1980s that contributed to certain elements of the Economic Recovery Program (ERP) success.[16]

In the case of Uganda, it was found that foreign aid boosted government expenditure by 80 percent of the amount of aid. The boost was even greater in the case of grants to agriculture (87 percent) and education (83 percent). It was also found that monitoring tended to enhance the extent to which foreign aid translated into higher government expenditure.[17]

One other important finding in the case study on Uganda is that aid has become more fungible over time. This may be partly related to the higher amounts of program aid in overall aid flows and partly related to the increase in the number of aid donors, which the authors argue, make it more difficult for individual donors to monitor what their aid is really used to finance. It appears that as the number of donors increases, aid is more likely to become fungible. That aid is partially fungible has policy implications in favor of aid coordination and the need to pay greater attention to the quality of the overall public expenditure program of recipient countries. It also underlines the importance of enhancing the capacity for budget management.

These findings suggest that it is very challenging to assess the differential impact of the types of aid (project, program, technical assistance) on aid dependence, as defined here. The fungibility of aid can obscure the "real" uses of any particular aid expenditure. More refined data may overcome this problem, but that is beyond the scope of this study.

. . . .

AID DEPENDENCE AND DEBT IN AFRICA

■   THE HIGH BURDEN OF DEBT CARRIED by a number of African countries has created a peculiar aspect of aid dependence in the region, as shown in Table 2. Debt as a proportion of GNP in Africa was nearly double the average for all developing countries.[18] With devaluation in the economic reform period—and for the CFA (Communaute Financiere Africaine) Franc Zone since 1994—the debt burden has increased considerably. Such a large stock of debt represents a claim on future resources and can discourage prospective investors. Debt service payments as a proportion of export earnings equaled just under 15 percent in Africa in 1998—less by several percentage points than the average for developing countries worldwide but still a considerable claim on the scarce resources of these mostly poor countries. Roughly half the $10.8 billion was paid in debt servicing in 1998 to bilateral and multilateral aid donors.

Foreign aid provided in the form of concessional loans unavoidably creates debt. The large amount of aid loans to many African countries over the past several decades has created large debt overhangs and significant debt servicing obligations. On one hand, the poor growth performance of most of these countries has made debt servicing a severe burden. On the other hand, the debt burden itself has been shown to be deleterious to growth. For instance, using 1970-1986 data, researchers found that annual economic growth (in a sample of 29 countries in Africa) is lowered by an average of 1.1 percent if a country is classified as high-debt.[19] This translates to about one-third of the sample mean gross domestic product (GDP) growth rate of Africa. The reduction of growth works via reduced productivity of investments. In a more recent study on debt burden and economic growth in 35 African countries, it was found that net outstanding debt was deleterious to economic growth for given levels of production inputs.[20] It was estimated that growth in Africa during the 1980s would have been 50 percent higher without the external debt burden, measured as net debt (total outstanding debt less total reserves).

However, it is in the interests of both the aid agencies (the creditors) and the African governments (the debtors) to avoid nonpayment of the debt and accumulation of arrears. Thus, bilateral aid agencies have agreed to a series of debt rescheduling and cancellations. Multilateral aid agencies like the World Bank have tended to continue to lend to heavily indebted countries with the realization that a significant number of their loans are in effect being used to repay past debts. This arrangement has created a peculiar dependence on the part of African debtors on foreign aid inflows to service their debts (and a dependence on the part of aid agencies—who do not want to have to report defaults on their loans—on financing those repayments with

	Africa	Least Developed Countries
TABLE 2. AFRICAN DEBT INDICATORS, 1998		
Debt as % of GNP	68	37
Debt as % of Export Earnings	232	146
Debt Servicing as % of Export Earnings	15	18

Source: World Bank, *Global Development Finance, Analysis and Summary Tables,* (Washington DC: World Bank, 1999), pp.188-9, 200-1.

continuing aid flows). The finding that nearly half the aid was used in effect to service external debts suggests that much of the aid was essentially a pass through—from the donor, through the African recipient, and then on to the external creditor (which was often also the donor). Thus, Africans are receiving significantly less aid *for their development* than the overall aid figures suggest. This is a peculiarity of aid dependence in heavily indebted poor countries like those in Africa.

To sum up, the intensity of aid gives us a general sense of the likely degree of aid dependence in Africa. The analysis in this chapter suggests that while aid dependence may not be as severe as suggested by data on aid intensity and has declined in recent years, it is still likely to be significant in the region and certainly higher than the degree of aid dependence in other parts of the developing world.

Armed with a definition of aid dependence and a broad sense of its extent in Africa, we now turn to the causes and consequences of that dependence.

NOTES

[1] This study will use the term "dependence" rather than "dependency." Although these terms are defined and often used interchangeably, the latter has been used in social science discourse (i.e., "dependency" theorists) to denote a particular set of international economic and often

political relationships. To avoid confusion, we shall avoid using the latter term except when referring to publications where dependency rather than dependence has been used.

[2] The Development Assistance Committee (DAC) of the Organization for Economic Cooperation and Development defines ODA as public resource transfers to poor countries with a major goal of supporting development and with a grant element of at least 25 percent in current value.

[3] Studies falling into this category include Roger Riddell, "Aid Dependence" in *Aid Dependency* (Stockholm: Swedish International Development Cooperation Agency, 1996). Riddell defines aid dependency as "that process by which the continued provision of aid appears to be making no significant contribution to the achievement of self-sustaining development." This definition appears to identify aid dependency with ineffective aid. (However, the indicators of aid dependency suggested by the author involve aid flows of various types relative to other economic indicators and do not include measures of effectiveness.)

[4] For example, Howard White and Robert Lensink define aid dependence as a situation in which a country needs external assistance to achieve a desired objective in the foreseeable future. See Robert Lensink and Howard White, "Aid Dependence: Issues and Indicators," report prepared for the Expert Group on Development Issues of the Swedish Ministry of Foreign Affairs, October 1997, mimeo. A similar approach to defining aid dependence was also taken by Robert Cassen and Machekeo Nissanke, "The Macroeconomics of Aid Dependence," World Bank Symposium on African External Finance in the 1990s, World Bank, Washington, DC, 1990, mimeo.

[5] This synthesis essay will focus entirely on the governments receiving aid; it does not include nongovernmental organizations (NGOs), which also receive an increasing amount of foreign assistance (estimated by the DAC at $1 billion in 1997 worldwide or 2 percent of total aid flows).

[6] K.Y. Amoako and Ali Ali, "Financing Development in Africa: Some Exploratory Results," framework paper prepared for ODC/AERC Project on Managing a Smooth Transition from Aid Dependence in Africa, 1998. The amount of external financing estimated to be needed for reducing poverty and eventually aid dependence in Africa would be $102 billion for the years 1999-2000, $84 billion for the period 2000-06, and $41 billion for the years 2006-10. These estimates assume high domestic savings rates and incremental capital output ratios. The authors did not foresee this amount of aid being available.

[7] See, for example, Peter Bauer, *Equality, the Third World and the Economic Delusion* (Cambridge, MA: Harvard University Press, 1981); or Elliot Berg, "Dilemmas in Donor Aid Strategies," prepared for Workshop on External Resources for Development, Netherlands Economic Institute, Rotterdam, May 1996.

[8] Stephen O'Connell and Charles Soludo, "Aid Intensity in Africa," framework paper prepared for the ODC/AERC Project on Managing a Smooth Transition from Aid Dependence in Africa, November 1998, p. 1.

[9] DAC, *Development Cooperation 1998* (Paris: OECD, 1999), pp. A61-62.

[10] We want to thank Alan Gelb and K.Y. Amoako for pointing out this connection among aid, project finance, and aid dependence in Africa.

[11] DAC, *Development Cooperation 1999* (Paris: OECD, 2000), Table 30, p. 226.

[12] World Bank, "Special Program of Assistance—Phase Five Towards New Aid Relationship," draft report (Washington, DC: World Bank, 1999), p. 28.

[13] World Bank, "Special Program of Assistance," op. cit. note 12.

[14] See Shantayanan Devarajan, Andrew Sunil Rajkumar, and Vinaya Swaroop, "What Does Aid to Africa Finance?" framework paper prepared for AERC/ODC Project on Managing a Smooth Transition from Aid Dependence in Africa, October 1998, mimeo.

[15] Devarajan, Rajkumar, and Swaroop, "What Does Aid to Africa Finance?" op. cit. note 14, p. 16.

[16] Samuel Wangwe, Peter Noni, and Deo Mutalemwa, "Managing the Transition from Aid Dependence: The Case Study on Tanzania," case study prepared for the ODC/AERC Project on Managing a Smooth Transition from Aid Dependence in Africa, 1999, mimeo.

[17] Germina Ssemogerere and William Kalema, "Managing the Transition from Aid Dependency in SSA: Opportunities and Challenges in Uganda," case study prepared for the ODC/AERC Project on Managing a Smooth Transition from Aid Dependence in Africa, 2000, mimeo.

[18] The data in this section are drawn from World Bank, *Global Development Finance*, country tables (Washington, DC: World Bank, 1999).

[19] Augustin Kwasi Fosu, "The Impact of External Debt on Economic Growth in Sub-Saharan Africa," *Journal of Economic Development*, Vol. 21, No. 1 (1996).

[20] Augustin Kwasi Fosu, "The External Debt Burden and Economic Growth in the 1980s: Evidence from Sub-Saharan Africa," *Canadian Journal of Development Studies*, Vol. XX, No. 2 (1999).

Chapter 2
The Causes and Consequences of Aid Dependence

Africa includes the largest number of the most highly aid dependent countries in the world. What is the explanation for this phenomenon? And what have been the consequences of Africa's dependence on foreign aid? The first part of this chapter addresses the first of these questions. The second part explores the consequences of aid dependence on African institutions, on African economies, and ultimately on African development.

. . . .

THE SOURCES OF AID DEPENDENCE IN AFRICA

■ FOREIGN AID INVOLVES THE PROVISION OF RESOURCES to governments and other entities that they would not otherwise have, to enable them to undertake a set of activities not possible in the absence of aid. In theory, aid for development should be provided to governments[1] committed to promoting equitable growth within their own countries, to help expand infrastructure, increase education and health services, reform the policies, strengthen institutions, and finance a host of other activities that contribute to economic and social progress. As governments put into place the physical and human infrastructure, adopt the policies, and create the institutional capacity necessary to sustain development, private investment (domestic and foreign) is expected to rise, expanding employment, national income, production, and government revenues. Sustained growth will, over time, usually lead to a reduction in poverty. The need for external concessional assistance will consequently diminish, and aid for development will eventually be eliminated. This has been the approximate path to reducing aid dependence followed by Costa Rica, South Korea, Taiwan, and Tunisia. It has not, however, been the path followed by most African countries. In Africa, foreign aid rose significantly from 1975 to 1994—both in absolute terms and relative to the size of African economies. At the same time, investment, savings, and growth have lagged in most of the region. The high level of aid dependence in much of Africa is the immediate result of high and rising aid levels combined with slow growth, continuing over an extended period of time. Let us examine each of these sources in more detail, starting with slow growth.

According to a recent World Bank report, *Can Africa Claim the 21st Century?*, there are three sets of explanations for slow growth in Africa:[2]

- Large terms of trade shocks offsetting increase in aid flows. A sharp increase in aid transfers to the non-oil exporting countries in Africa after 1970 was mostly offset by terms of trade losses. The rest was more than offset by increases in external debt;

- Poor governance; and

- Low levels of human resource development.

These deficiencies have discouraged the savings and investment necessary to sustain economic growth and reduce poverty over the long term. Further, in a number of African countries, failures of governance (including gross corruption and incompetence, and exclusion and repression of opposition) have also fed discontent among differing regional, religious, or ethnic groups. Those groups, often supported by outside powers or commercial interests, have turned to violence, warlordism, and civil war, causing a collapse in the state and a destruction of lives and economic assets.

Other factors contributing to Africa's poor growth performance include the difficult physical environment: the tropical climate (with its exceptional disease load), the limited resource bases of many countries, the small size of many economies, the numerous landlocked countries, and the "neighborhood effect" on potentially good economic performers unable to attract investment because they are surrounded by poor economic performers, collapsed states, or civil wars. Exogenous shocks have also played a role: volatile world prices for the primary products on which African countries depend for their export earnings, and erratic rainfall which often produces droughts in the more arid countries. Further, the adverse movement in the terms of trade of most African countries in the late 1970s and early 1980s (in many countries amounting to losses larger than aid inflows), together with the accumulated problems of economic mismanagement, produced a severe balance-of-payments and debt crisis, helping to depress economic growth throughout the 1980s into the 1990s. Economic reforms and an improvement in primary product prices have helped boost the growth performance of a number of countries in the mid-1990s. The continuation of low levels of saving and investment have meant that overall growth in the region has remained positive but modest, seldom exceeding 5 percent per year for an extended period of time. Despite hopes for an imminent African economic renaissance, economic prospects confronting the region at the end of the 1990s were modest at best, with declining commodity prices and a rising propensity toward conflict in parts of the region.

RISING AID LEVELS

Figure 1 shows the overall flow of aid from bilateral and multilateral donors to Sub-Saharan Africa from 1970 to 1997. Aid to Africa increased rapidly during the 1980s—especially during the latter part of that decade. It reached a peak in the early 1990s and has trended downward since that time. Data for 1997 and 1998 show the continuation of a decline in aid to the region.

Several factors explain this trend in aid flows to the region. Donors have aided African countries for a variety of reasons. For many donor governments, the Cold War was a factor in the size of their flows. The Cold War intensified in Africa in the late 1970s and early 1980s (with Soviet gains in the Horn and in parts of southern Africa), and Western aid flows rose accordingly.

But aid was not only provided as a tool in the Cold War. Aid levels also responded to perceived economic needs, leading to increasing aid allocations, especially from Nordic countries, the Netherlands, and other governments and international organizations less driven by Cold War diplomacy. Africa had been the least developed of all major world regions from the independence period in the 1960s, and many donors saw it then and continued to regard it as among the world's most important development challenges. The deepening economic crisis and the initiation of structural adjustment programs provided important justifications for rising amounts of assistance during the 1980s.

By the mid-1990s, several factors led to a decrease in aid levels. The end of the Cold War removed one of the principle justifications for aid to Africa for a number of countries, most prominently the United States. As the security rationale for aid diminished, its relevance to major foreign policy goals among donors lessened, and those donors began to take a closer look at the effectiveness of their aid in Africa. They found that their aid there

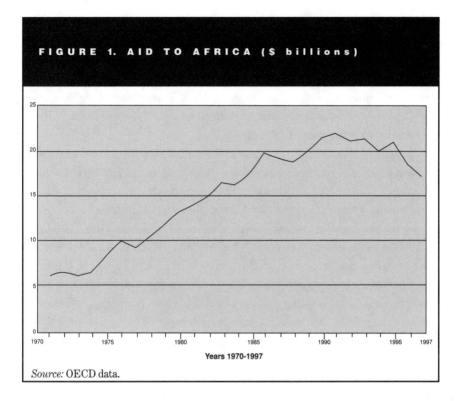

FIGURE 1. AID TO AFRICA ($ billions)

Source: OECD data.

was the least effective of aid to any major world region and that the projects their aid financed often proved unsustainable.[3] At a minimum, the poor performance of aid in Africa began to make it difficult to argue for larger aid flows.

Another factor leading to a decrease in overall aid levels and aid to Africa in particular has been the fiscal problems of aid-giving governments. Efforts in the mid-1990s by the U.S. government to reduce its fiscal deficit, by the Europeans to meet the terms of Maastricht for participation in the European Monetary Union, and by the Japanese government to deal with its prolonged economic recession led to a reduction in aid on the part of most of these governments.

Finally, in the early 1990s, another major claimant for concessional assistance appeared: the former socialist bloc countries that had begun to shift to free markets and democracy. Aid to these countries rose quickly in the early 1990s and remains high as a number of them continue to struggle to complete their economic and political transitions. By the end of the decade, aid funding for those former socialist countries having made good progress toward economic and political transitions was tapering off. But a further demand for aid arose in the wartorn Balkans, to the countries affected by the Asian financial crisis, and later to East Timor, requiring donors to increase their aid for those unfortunate countries and regions or to divert funds from existing programs.

As of this writing, the latest DAC statistics on foreign aid worldwide show a 9 percent increase in 1998 over the level in 1997 but a continuing decrease in aid to Africa. Several of the major donor governments—including Canada, France, Germany, and Sweden—show decreases in their overall aid levels. And the United States, with one of the largest increases in aid in 1998, was responding to emergency needs in Central America and the Balkans. It seemed likely that the increase in U.S. aid was temporary—indeed, Congress appeared likely to cut U.S. foreign aid during 2000 below the President's request (not counting emergency supplements) and the outcome of bargaining between the two branches of the U.S. government was still uncertain in late summer.

These factors explain why aid donors provided relatively large amounts of aid to African countries over several decades and why that aid now is decreasing. It does not explain why African governments sought and accepted large quantities of assistance in the first place. The immediate answer is that they were poor and needed assistance to spur their growth and development. Concessional assistance is useful for rapid growth while also enabling increased consumption to reduce poverty. But this is only part of the answer. Aid relationships must be conducive to aid effectiveness. After all, African governments ceded much of the authority and responsibility to the donors for the use of the aid and almost never rejected the aid regardless of whether its proposed uses fit their development goals. As a result, what was created was a "donor-driven" aid relationship. We shall explore the details of this relationship in the section on the "aid regimes" below. The question here is what agendas other than development did the aid fulfill for the Africans?

As with many of the donors of aid to Africa, the nondevelopmental agendas of African governments were primarily political. Aid provided African officials with additional resources that could bolster the patronage-based politics on which most of their regimes were based—a new aid-financed vehicle for one client, a trip abroad for training or a conference for another, new employment for a third, a village development project for a fourth, additional procurement contracts for another, and so on. But patronage was not the only political value of the aid. What is often overlooked is the symbolic function of aid. Aid is a voluntary transfer of resources from one government to another. Explicitly and often implicitly, it symbolizes approbation by the former for the latter. Gaining aid from major powers or important international institutions is frequently seen in Africa as a sign that the recipient government has powerful friends (some of which may come to its aid in the event of internal or external security threats) and is influential in encouraging those friends to provide it with resources.

Another symbolic function of aid in Africa has been its "promise" of development. Additional concessional resources are often characterized by governments and viewed by publics as a harbinger of economic progress and welcomed as such. No one has captured this symbolic function of aid better than former Tanzanian President, Julius Nyerere:

> Our government and different groups of our leaders never stop thinking about methods of getting finance from abroad. And if we get some money, or even if we just get a promise of it, our newspapers, our radio, and our leaders, all advertise the fact in order that every person shall know that salvation is coming, or is on the way. . . . Even when we have merely started discussions with a foreign government or institution for a gift, a loan or a new industry, we make an announcement—even though we do not know the outcome of the discussions. Why do we do all this? Because we want people to know that we have started discussions which will bring prosperity.[4]

In short, the causes of aid dependence in Africa are diverse: the real economic needs of African governments for resources to further their development and the efforts of aid donors to assist that development and respond to deepening economic crisis; the political and bureaucratic imperatives of aid donors to advance their broader diplomatic objectives and to expand overall aid levels and allocate all available aid monies within the time they were available to be spent; and the political goals of Africans to increase resources available for patronage and benefit from the various symbolic advantages that foreign aid provides.

These are the major explanations of the rise of aid dependence in Africa. But what kind of "aid regime" developed out of these motivations?

An aid regime is the set of norms, principles, rules, and decision-making procedures that shape the behavior of the donors and recipients of foreign aid. What are the characteristics of the aid regime in Africa and how has it evolved over the past four decades?

One important characteristic of the aid environment in Africa is the large and growing number of aid donors; approximately 40 governments and international aid agencies are active in providing aid in most African countries. (There are typically hundreds of NGOs also providing various types of aid in these countries, but we shall not include them in this analysis.) Second, the desire for aid on the part of African governments and the desire to provide that aid on the part of donors have created what is in essence a bargaining relationship between the donors and the African recipient, with neither side having all the bargaining power all the time. Thus, aid donors have not always been able to dictate the terms of aid to Africans, while Africans have usually been reluctant to reject outright the wishes of aid donors.

Within these parameters, what sorts of norms and patterns of behavior involving the management of aid have evolved and with what impact on aid dependence in Africa? Nicolas van de Walle, in his paper for this project, entitled "Managing Aid in Africa: The Rise and Decline of the Structural Adjustment Regime," identifies two regimes that have shaped the delivery of aid in the region: one based on a "planning paradigm"; the other on structural adjustment.

The planning paradigm, prevalent during the 1960s and 1970s, was encouraged by aid donors, which often required that governments receiving their aid create three- to five-year, formal indicative development plans. Donors would then attempt to fill the resource gaps in those plans by providing funding for projects not likely to be financed by private investors (e.g., expanding social services and infrastructure) and for technical assistance to strengthen African institutions and to expand the "absorptive capacity" of African governments for managing aid and other resources effectively.

By the 1970s, donors were no longer insisting on development plans. Those that had been produced had tended to be weak, with few priorities and based on poor data. Nearly all African governments were receiving aid from several and often dozens of aid donors, regardless of their economic performance. An increasing number of donors, with rising amounts of aid to be disbursed, began to deal directly with spending ministries in recipient countries. In addition, the donors often set up and staffed parallel organizations, associated with but semi-independent of African governments, enabling these parallel organizations to implement their aid projects quickly and effectively.

The planning paradigm—or what was left of it by the end of the 1970s—gave way to the "adjustment regime" of the 1980s and 1990s. This aid regime arose as a result of the severe debt and foreign exchange crisis experienced by African governments at the end of the 1970s, with the rise in prices for petroleum and manufactured goods imports and the decline in the prices of the primary products that made up the exports of most African countries. (The collapse in the price of petroleum in 1982 added African oil exporters to the countries in economic crisis.) While aid donors continued to fund large numbers of projects in Africa, the focus of their attention and a rising proportion of their aid were allocated to support structural adjustment. This involved aid (to be used to fund needed imports or debt servicing) conditioned on economic reforms, typically involving currency devaluation, decreases in government budget deficits, stricter control on credit, elimination of price controls and other economic regulations, privatization of state-owned enterprises, and a host of other reforms in agriculture, education, health, finance, and the civil service.

The multilateral aid agencies—above all, the World Bank and the International Monetary Fund (IMF), which is not an aid agency but provided highly concessional resources for stabilization in poor countries during the 1990s—played an increasingly prominent role in the structural adjustment regime: in conceptualizing the policy problems to be addressed, in providing loans and mobilizing funding from other donors, and in coordinating aid donors to support structural adjustment programs. The World Bank also actively sought allies within African governments (usually ministers of finance and/or central bank governors) who supported economic reforms.

It appears that the heyday of the structural adjustment regime is now past. Some reforms—especially those that are relatively simple administratively to implement (like exchange rate adjustments) or the political costs of which are widely disbursed or fall on the less politically influential segments of the population (such as price decontrols)—have been widely adopted in Africa. The more complex institutional reforms—such as privatization or those that fall heavily on powerful political elites, like financial sector and civil service reforms—have been far less widely adopted. Donors have recognized that using conditioned lending, in effect, to force African governments to implement such reforms, is not likely to have a high success rate. Thus, while not abandoning the notion of aid tied to reforms, donors have begun to explore ways to reshape the way they do business. While the new regime that appears to be emerging as yet lacks a name, it involves commitments on the part of aid donors to four elements: selectivity, participation, ownership, and developing new modalities for managing the aid. These elements are being shaped within the broad conceptual context of the Comprehensive Development Framework (CDF), proposed by the World Bank. The CDF is a template intended to include the numerous and diverse elements—economic, political, social, even cultural—that can play a role in development, broadly defined. Following on the CDF and international poverty reduction goals agreed in the DAC in 1995, a number of developing countries, with the support of the World Bank, have also produced Poverty Reduction Strategies to guide government policies and investments (including aid-funded investments).

"Selectivity" refers to an approach to aid allocations that takes into account the quality of governance, the commitment to development, and the capacity of recipient governments. During the Cold War, large amounts of aid for political or commercial reasons were provided to governments that were corrupt or highly incompetent. That practice seems much less in evidence today. Aid has diminished significantly to several countries that donors perceived as having the most corrupt, incompetent, or repressive governments, for example, the Democratic Republic of the Congo, Kenya, and Zimbabwe. (Even with the decreases in their aid during the 1990s, these governments received $1.7 billion, or just over 10 percent of net ODA to Africa in 1997.)[5] However, the implementation of a policy of selectivity on the part of aid donors still leaves much to be desired. For a number of governments with serious problems of corruption, repression, and economic mismanagement—for example, Togo or Cameroon—aid has remained stable or has risen since 1993.

"Ownership" of aid programs and projects refers to the sense of engagement and responsibility on the part of individuals and groups in recipient countries for making aid-funded activities work. "Participation" is another word often attaching to ownership; it usually refers to consultations on planned aid activities by officials of aid agencies with key government officials and with civil society organizations in African countries. Sometimes it refers to joint planning and execution of aid projects, although this appears to be far less common. Coincident with this latter emphasis has been an increase in the number of NGOs (both Northern and Southern) working on development projects in African countries. Ownership, while obviously important, still lacks the clarity necessary for effective policy implementation. Participation is increasing, but the extent and impact on the effectiveness of aid and on ownership is as yet unclear.

During the period of economic reforms, many countries made improvements in the soundness of their macroeconomic policies but at the same time undercut ownership of the policy agenda. Many countries under the policy reform programs paid so much attention to meeting targets agreed between them and the multilateral financial institutions that the policymaking process became a collaborative effort in principle, but in practice the recipient countries became more dependent on these institutions. Thus, the recipient countries increasingly lost their grip on their own policymaking process. For instance, five-year plans were suspended, and shorter-term economic recovery programs took their place. Policymaking reflected more the "Washington Consensus" than the wishes of stakeholders in recipient countries. From the point of view of the recipient countries, this was a way of facilitating agreement in the negotiations with the multilateral institutions, without which, it was perceived, the flow of aid not only from multilateral donors but also from bilateral donors would be put at risk. The outcome was considerable erosion of ownership of the policy agenda.

In response to these problems, new modalities involving the management and delivery of aid have been developed. Specifically, there is an increasing emphasis on the part of donors on Sector Investment Programs (SIPs). Ideally, a SIP has the following characteristics. Recipient governments take the leadership in developing sectoral policies and strategies, in consultation with their own bureaucracy and populations and with external donors. They also develop medium-term projections of resource availability, needs, and spending plans and priorities, also in consultation with external donors. The latter then collaborate in providing the government with needed funding, usually over a multi-year period, to realize its goals and priorities. In doing this, donors should harmonize their procedures (for example, the disbursement of funds, procurement, accounting, and other forms of evaluation) and, if possible, pool their resources to provide budget support for the SIP. Both donors and the recipient government agree on the outcomes they are trying to achieve and indicators of progress toward those outcomes. Donors then monitor government expenditures to ensure they follow the agreed plan and that the expected outcomes are being achieved.

This approach is intended to provide more coherent, efficient, and more effective aid, especially where that aid is large and provided by multiple donors. But it also has costs for both donors and recipients. Aid donors give up the ability to attribute particular activities and outcomes to their assistance (through funding projects or reform programs) in exchange for a say in the government's overall sector plans, priorities, and expenditures. The recipient government gives up a measure of control over its sectoral plans and expenditures for more efficient aid inflows and multi-year aid commitments.

Additionally, in the particular sector to be aided, a SIP requires leadership and capacity on the part of the recipient government—in particular, the sectoral ministry involved—to develop the sectoral policies, strategies, and expenditure plans and to make them available to their own people and external aid donors for consultation and negotiation. Experience in several African countries—for example, with developing health sector development programs in Ghana and Zambia—shows that this process can take two to three years. It also requires aid agencies to exercise patience and discipline on their part to collaborate with each other and the government, rather than negotiating individually with ministries on aid projects as they have done in the past. It can also require considerable staff time on the part of both government ministries and aid donors not only to examine the government's strategies and plans but also to monitor the implementation of those plans. The government's performance in a SIP will likely involve periodic reviews by donors, perhaps several times per year. (This has been the approach in a number of SIPs.) Government for its part will have to be transparent (often far more so than it is accustomed to being) in its expenditures in the sector. The use of public funds for patronage or personal gain will provoke objections by vigilant donors.

How widely have SIPs been applied in Sub-Saharan Africa? And with what impact? At least 17 African countries have had SIPs in such sectors as roads, health, education, agriculture, energy, water, and the urban sector.[6] By 1998, it was anticipated that one-quarter of World Bank lending in Africa would be in the form of SIPs.[7]

An effort to assess progress under four SIPs showed that most had been useful in helping the government gain information and a measure of control over the multiple donors operating in various sectors in its country.[8] (In Mozambique, it was discovered, there were 164 aid donors—including NGOs—operating in the health sector independently of one another and to a considerable extent, of the ministry of health.) Government ministries showed leadership and capacity in designing strategies for their sectors. But there were capacity problems in most cases in carrying out those strategies, especially where local governments were involved. SIPs threaten to centralize decision making and to jeopardize decentralization and broad participation in development management. In several cases, donors were reluctant to coordinate or pool their financing—at times, because they were uncertain of the financial capacity and probity of government ministries.

These preliminary findings suggested that SIPs were potentially highly useful, albeit challenging to implement by both donors and recipients. A later study by the Africa Region of the World Bank emphasized the importance of ensuring that government ministries involved in SIPs have the requisite capacity and assessing that capacity before a SIP is planned.[9] Despite these caveats, SIPs appear to be part of the emerging aid regime—particularly in countries with governmental competence, capacity, and commitment to improve the well-being of their people. This study also found that in regard to donor collaboration in planning and implementing SIPs, a number of donors remained resistant to harmonizing policies—for example, procurement processes—and pooling of resources.

How shall we conceptualize the new aid regime that appears to be taking shape in Africa? If both aid donors and African recipients realize their stated goals, there will be a more balanced and responsible aid regime in the region in which donors are more selective and coordinated and in which Africans take a more prominent role in deciding on the use of the aid and in managing it. There will also be a greater emphasis on aid for social sector activities. However, it is too soon to say whether this more responsible and hopefully more effective aid regime will become a reality or whether the past practices of both donors and recipients in the allocation, use, and management of aid will continue into the future regardless of the rhetoric of responsibility.

THE IMPACT OF AID DEPENDENCE
ON AFRICAN ECONOMIES

■   FOREIGN AID PROVIDES RECIPIENTS WITH RESOURCES additional to those available in the absence of the aid. Those additional resources permit recipients to make expenditures—for consumption, investment, or servicing debt—not otherwise possible. The increased expenditures can have a positive impact on growth, for example, by expanding investments or increasing the demand for domestic products through funding increases in consumption. Large aid expenditures over an extended period of time can also have negative effects on recipient economies—causing the "Dutch disease," depressing taxes and savings and crowding out investment. A high volatility in the flow of aid to aid-dependent countries can also disrupt economic planning and management and depress growth. Where aid makes a positive contribution to growth over an extended period, the need for aid eventually diminishes and aid will have been effective in accomplishing its task regardless of any negative effects. Where aid is not effective, the overall economic impact of aid dependence may be negative and, to the extent that the debt was provided in the form of credits, will leave that debt to be repaid. Let us examine what we know about each of the effects in turn.

THE DUTCH DISEASE

High levels of aid can affect a country's real exchange rate and, through that, the competitiveness of its exports. The Dutch disease, which can be caused by sudden increases in aid (or other resource inflows, for example, from windfall earnings from exports), typically leads to an increase in expenditures on domestic, nontradable goods. That increase can fuel inflation, which in turn leads to an appreciation of the exchange rate and a decrease in the competitiveness of a country's exports. The export sector is often among the more dynamic sectors and widely viewed as key to growth. A shift of resources away from this sector can, therefore, dampen economic growth.[10] There is some empirical evidence for a negative relationship between high levels of aid and the performance of nontraditional exports. The preliminary results of a study by Ibrahim Elbadawi (using panel data for

62 developing countries, including 28 from Africa) found that the relationship between the level of foreign aid and the size of nontraditional exports resembled a "Laffer Curve," in which aid and the export level rose together to a peak and then with further increases in aid, exports of nontraditional exports declined.[11] (The peak or threshold above which a negative relationship between aid and nontraditional export levels appeared was when aid reached 22 percent of GNP.) This study is suggestive of relationships between aid and trade, but it is highly aggregated. More work will be necessary to enable us to analyze and predict these relationships for African economies.

THE TAX EFFORT

There has long been a debate among economists on the relationship between high levels of foreign aid and the tax effort of recipient countries. It has been argued that aid dependence can act as a disincentive for governments to collect optimal levels of taxes since the aid inflows relieve governments of the often politically painful and administratively complicated tasks of imposing and collecting taxes. However, there are differences in opinions among economists regarding the optimal level of taxes in Sub-Saharan Africa. Several IMF officials find that a much greater effort would be appropriate,[12] whereas Paul Collier of the World Bank argues that it would be unwise for Africans to extract more taxes, given the likely disincentive effect of such taxes on trade and investment.[13] On the relationship between aid and tax efforts in Africa and elsewhere, empirical studies have produced contradictory results. Howard White, in a 1994 study of aid and tax efforts worldwide, found that aid in general tended to reduce tax efforts.[14] In contrast, in a paper for this project, Shanta Devarajan et al. found that aid did not reduce the tax efforts of the 18 countries in their sample.[15] Here again, there is a need for further empirical research to provide definitive conclusions on the impact of aid (and aid dependence) and tax efforts in Africa.

SAVINGS

A review of research on aid and savings carried out by Azam and Fouda concluded that most studies found a negative impact of aid on the rate of savings.[16] Case studies undertaken for this project found a positive correlation between aid and savings in Uganda and Burkina Faso. In Mali and Ethiopia, no significant impact of aid on savings was found. Here again more research is required.

CROWDING OUT INVESTMENT

In theory, foreign aid should complement and encourage higher levels of investment by strengthening the environment in which private agents can earn profitable returns from risking their resources. However, some have argued that foreign aid can crowd out private investment. This can occur if recipient governments, in coming up with the counterpart funds needed to match aid inflows, increase their expenditures through borrowing from the banking system, making credit scarce and discouraging private investors. (A significant expansion in government expenditures can also be financed through higher taxes or credit creation. Either of these alternatives can also discourage private investors.) What has been the experience worldwide and in Sub-Saharan Africa?

Where the policy environment is supportive of economic investment, an extra dollar of aid has been found to increase investment by nearly double the amount of the aid. (This finding is based on a study of aid worldwide.)[17] Further, in poor countries recovering from war or severe economic crisis, aid to finance basic public goods is needed to create the minimal preconditions for investment, economic recovery, and healthy growth rates achieved. In effect, the impact of aid dependence on private investment is influenced by the overall economic environment and the taxation and credit policies of governments. Where conditions are supportive, some have argued that greater aid dependence can give a significant boost to investment and growth: aid should "taper in" before it "tapers out."[18] The experience of Botswana is just such a case. There, aid was important in helping the government expand education and health services for the population, to fund geological explorations, and later to construct the infrastructure needed to attract foreign investment in the country's rich natural resources (especially diamonds). The subsequent investments in diamonds and other minerals greatly expanded the country's income and the revenues of the government, and eventually reduced the need for and dependence on foreign aid.

In Mozambique, foreign aid has been very large in recent years, providing humanitarian relief to many of the victims of war and helping them to begin the process of recovery. It has also supported an extensive economic reform program, involving the dismantling of the socialist state, including abandonment of central planning, liberalization of controls on prices of most domestic goods and services, trade liberalization, labor market liberalization, exchange rate adjustments, extensive privatization, and liberalization of financial markets and regulations governing private investment. These aid-supported policies may well open the way to a tapering in of investment in Mozambique—indeed, a large aluminum smelter is already in the process of implementation.

In Tanzania and Zambia, where policy and institutional environments have been weak, large aid inflows and an extended period of aid dependence have not been associated with a tapering in of investment. In Zambia, an econometric analysis done for this research project showed only a minor association between aid and investment.

VOLATILITY IN AID

A further potential impact of aid dependence on economic performance in African countries involves the variability in aid levels. Where economies are heavily dependent on a particular source of revenues (whether they be in the form of foreign export earnings or portfolio investment) and where those revenues have the tendency to vary significantly, economic management becomes considerably more difficult and the potential for serious economic disruptions arises. Lensink and Morrissey found that when uncertainty of aid is taken into account, aid is found to have a significant positive effect on growth, largely due to its effect on the volume of investment.[19] The finding that uncertainty reduces the effectiveness of aid is robust. This suggests that stability in donor-recipient relationships could enhance aid effectiveness, by making it easier for recipients to predict future aid flows that may in turn permit more investment and better fiscal planning.

How volatile have aid flows been in Africa and is there evidence that they have had a negative impact on economic management and performance there? A recent study by Paul Collier found that aid flows to Africa are actually more stable than other sources of government revenue, and, further, that aid levels tend to vary inversely with changes in revenue flows—i.e., that they reduce rather than increase the overall volatility of resource flows to African governments.[20] This finding suggests that the volatility in aid flows does not tend to be a significant problem of aid dependence.

. . . .

THE POTENTIAL IMPACT OF AID DEPENDENCE ON AFRICAN INSTITUTIONS[21]

■   THE KEY FINDING OF THE RESEARCH PROJECT on which this essay is based is that institutions matter in mediating the impact of aid dependence. Foreign aid, provided in relatively large amounts over an extended period of time, can strengthen or weaken the institutions (including both the organizations and the norms, principles, and patterns of behavior) in the countries receiving it. Aid can strengthen organizations by expanding the technical and administrative capacity of their staffs and by increasing their activities, which in turn can promote organizational learning and broader economic development, eventually obviating the need for foreign aid. But it can also weaken recipient country institutions by undercutting the planning, budgeting, administrative capacities, and general operations of recipient organizations and their political accountability and legitimacy. It can also reduce the sense of initiative and responsibility on the part of individuals in recipient organizations for achieving their goals and missions.

The difference between these two institutional outcomes of aid dependence turns on how the aid is managed by donors and recipients. Where the recipient government has been led by individuals committed to development and disciplined in their pursuit of it, and where recipient governments have had the capacity to manage the aid as well as coordinate the aid donors—as in the case of Botswana (more on this in the next chapter)—aid dependence has served to both strengthen institutions and spur development. In the numerous countries in Africa where this has not been the case, aid dependence has further weakened the organizations and processes necessary to manage an economy effectively (as well as foreign aid itself), as we shall see below.

Large flows of aid over an extended period of time in Africa have almost always permitted recipient governments to expand their activities beyond those they could fund from domestic resource mobilization. This is advantageous if governments implement policies and utilize their resources to promote the growth that will expand public revenues and obviate the need for aid in the future, as noted above. But combined with weak tax collection efforts in many African countries, generally poor economic management, and government policies that provided automatic employment for graduates in the public sector regardless of manpower needs or the capabilities of the graduates, foreign aid appears to have led many governments to expand services, wages, and employment without expanding the domestic economy or their tax revenues.

One of the most important potential impacts of aid dependence in Africa has been on the planning and budgeting systems of recipient governments. These systems, never strong, can be seriously undercut not only by the large flows of aid over an extended period but also by the way the aid is managed. Initially, the aid regime based on a "planning paradigm" likely encouraged African governments to attempt to survey their overall economic needs and long-term objectives and develop strategies for meeting them. But it appears that the capacity of those governments in the early decades of independence to undertake such a complex planning exercise (including the collection of reliable data, the modeling of their economies, as well as the difficult political process of identifying priorities) was limited.

Further, most African governments were unable or unwilling to require their multiple aid donors to fit projects and programs within their plans. As we have seen, they were, in effect, so eager for the aid that they were reluctant to reject it even when it did not correspond to local needs and priorities.

As the number of aid donors operating in individual African countries increased and their aid grew, the donors began to deal with individual government ministries to get their projects accepted. Not surprisingly, those ministries were eager to obtain the aid. The donors also typically required local counterpart financing for their aid projects, absorbing an increasing amount of the domestic revenues of those agencies and a commitment to assume responsibility for the recurrent costs of projects once aid had terminated. These processes undercut the abilities of African governments to plan and budget in a rational way and, in the end, left them with financial commitments they were unable to meet.

Aid donors, in a hurry to implement their aid projects, also began to bypass the African governments they were supposed to be aiding. Where governments were slow to undertake agreed projects or could not manage them adequately from the point of view of donors (or where corruption threatened to lead to the misappropriation of donor funds), many donors simply set up organizations separate from the line agencies to manage their projects or had their own officials placed in government agencies to do the same thing. These approaches further undercut the capacity and responsibility of government agencies for controlling their own affairs and learning from that responsibility. It also deprived the aid projects of a bureaucratic "home" once the aid was terminated. Many of them subsequently collapsed.

The influence of donors over the projects and spending patterns undertaken by individual ministries was extended to the economic policies of recipient governments with the emergence of the structural adjustment regime for aid, described above. Because of their urgent need for foreign exchange and debt relief and often their weak analytical capacity, African governments frequently ceded considerable influence over their economic policies to aid donors, led by now by the IMF and the World Bank. The economic crisis of the 1980s and the requirements faced by most African governments to cut back on expenditures (and on the size of their civil service) often served further to weaken governmental capacity as the more capable public servants left government for more lucrative jobs as consultants— often for aid agencies. Many of the policy reforms urged by aid donors were clearly necessary, but the way they were negotiated and implemented (when they were, in fact, implemented) and the way they neglected their impact on governmental capacity further served to weaken the capacity of African public organizations.

In several country case studies, it has been illustrated that a number of these problems persist. For instance, in Burkina Faso, Mozambique, Tanzania, and Zambia, a substantial proportion of foreign aid is not included in the government's budget. This makes it difficult for the government, the public, and aid donors to know for sure just how much aid the country is receiving, which in turn makes the effective management of those resources a challenge. Off-budget resources have produced another problem for the government: the recurrent costs of aid-funded projects create claims against future public resources that are not included in planning for revenues and expenditures by the government.

Another aspect of the various regimes in which foreign aid has been provided to African governments added to problems of capacity in those countries. The multiplicity of uncoordinated aid donors created serious transaction and coordination costs for African officials who had to receive senior officials from numerous aid agencies, attend conferences, try to implement (or at least, keep track of) the many aid projects of those donors (each with its own administrative and budgetary systems and cycles) while attempting to manage their ministries or agencies. The sheer number and diversity of aid donors often overtaxed senior African government officials who were also typically the key decision makers in their ministries.

The cases of Tanzania and Zambia exhibit these types of problems. The Government of Tanzania hesitated, for quite some time, to coordinate its numerous aid donors or, for that matter, to have the donors coordinate themselves, fearing that they might "gang up" on the government and force it to undertake policies it did not want. Recently, however, the Tanzanian government has relaxed its stance and shown commitment toward aid coordination. This development is an indication of greater trust and improved relationships between Tanzania and its development partners following discussions and agreements based on the 1995 reconciliatory study on aid relationships (the Helleiner Report).[22] That report made recommendations on how aid relationships could be improved. The report was discussed between Tanzania and its development partners and reached a 15-point agreement in 1997 and since then implementation of the agreed points has been followed in the annual Consultative Group meetings.

There was, in fact, a formal procedure within the Tanzanian government for managing its aid flows. The Ministry of Finance, the Treasury, and the Planning Commission were responsible for various aspects of the planning and implementation of aid within the government's overall development plans, but this procedure did not work. Coordination was ineffective, the budget of the government was not wholly transparent, governmental expenditures were frequently audited only years after they had been made, and individual ministries and agencies were left to deal directly with aid donors. Donors, for their part, often set up their own special project implementation units to ensure that their funds were used for the purposes intended and within the time frame prescribed. These practices, in turn, further eroded the ability of the Tanzanian government to plan and budget effectively. In the discussions and agreements following recommendations of the Helleiner Report, willingness to depart from this tradition has been clearly demonstrated.[23]

The management of aid in Zambia has also been problematical. The patterns of donor-driven aid—often uncoordinated with government priorities and outside government planning and budgeting frameworks as well as involving the imposition of excessive amounts of technical assistance—are evident in that country. Other problems of aid management in Zambia include a lack of adequate data on economic conditions in the country, weak analytical capacity and financial systems within the government, and competition among government agencies to take the lead in coordinating aid donors.

A final aspect of aid in Africa that complicated the functioning of recipient governments involves the amount and nature of technical assistance provided those governments. This assistance is frequently provided independently of government plans, priorities, or requests. (Donors have often required the acceptance of such assistance as a condition for their aid.) There seems almost to be a syndrome occurring in many countries in which weak governmental capacity and efforts to downsize the civil service lead to an increase in aid-funded technical assistance that replaces indigenous expertise and further reduces the capacity of government agencies to manage their own affairs effectively.[24] Indeed, the amount of technical assistance today, measured in the number of expatriate advisors funded by aid agencies, is larger than during the early decades of independence. These experiences have led a number of experts and African officials to view technical assistance more as part of the problem than the solution.

POLITICAL EFFICACY

Governments, to be effective, must be accountable to their people. Organizations, to be effective, must be accountable to those they serve. To ensure accountability, governments and organizations must have incentives to take into account the wishes of their clients. Competitive markets help ensure the accountability of private enterprises to those who purchase their products. Membership and the financial contributions of members often serve as vehicles of accountability for nonprofit organizations. Voters and those who represent them in legislative bodies promote the accountability of governments. In democratic systems and even in autocratic political systems, the necessity for governments to collect taxes (and the ability of citizens to "exit"—including tax avoidance) can act as a vehicle of their accountability.

Where organizations derive a significant proportion of their revenues from aid donors or other sources, their accountability will tend to shift to those sources, lessening their accountability to their populations. The high levels of aid to African governments over several decades have likely had just such an effect. In the case of Malawi, for example, a group of aid donors dubbed themselves the "board of directors," because the proportion of their aid relative to the budget of the government was so high and because both public and private groups and individuals turned to them so often to resolve pressing issues. A loss of accountability can undercut the incentives and the capacity for a government or organization to serve its clientele as the voices of those they are supposed to serve are drowned out by the voices of those who fund them. Anecdotal evidence suggests this is not an uncommon problem in aid dependent African countries.[25]

A major limitation of econometric studies examining the impact of aid is that they have often addressed aid in its aggregate, often without analyzing the type and composition of the aid. The composition of aid matters and has influenced shifts in forms of aid. Various studies of aid-specific projects and programs have shown that the form of aid does have an impact on effectiveness. The shift from project to program aid that has been observed in some countries in the 1980s is one response to evaluations showing that project aid was not working, especially as the recurrent budget allocations needed to effectively utilize the installed capacities became increasingly scarce. The effectiveness of technical assistance has also been put into question. Technical assistance has sometimes been associated with underutilization of local human resources and failure to build up local capacities. Project aid, administered in parallel administrative machineries, has often been associated with weakening of the already weak institutional capacities. The consequent displacement of local human resources and institutional distortions could not have been conducive to growth. In addition, concern has been voiced about the problem of packaging aid, and recipients have little choice to make in terms the aid components they really need. In particular, projects packaged with personnel and equipment like computers and vehicles have sometimes been accepted because of the equipment, even when technical assistance personnel were really not needed. To the extent that the composition of aid and its administration have had influence on the building or erosion of institutional and human capacities in the recipient countries, more research needs to be done on a disaggregated analysis of aid by its various types.

The framework papers and the case studies undertaken for this project point to one major finding: aid dependence in Africa, which has usually involved large numbers of aid donors, has helped development and reduced the need for aid in countries where the government had the ability and willingness to manage its economy *and the aid donors* in a coherent and disciplined manner—including the willingness to reject aid that did not fit into government plans and budgets.

This raises the question of the relationship between aid and policy. Azam and Fouda in their paper for this project have found that aid can amplify the benefits of a good policy package for a recipient government that pursues it. However, they also indicate that in the real world bilateral donors' interests have been a fundamental determinant of aid allocation, often offsetting the effect of good policy choice.[26]

The extent to which aid allocation has been able to induce good policies is not encouraging either. Burnside and Dollar performed an econometric investigation on this relationship and failed to find any significant effect of aid on policy on average.[27] Taking into account different contributions on the practice of conditionality, Azam and Fouda have provided further arguments in favor of an outcome-based conditionality as a means to optimize the economic impact of aid on recipients.

The relationship between aid and policy is complex. The approach adopted in the Burnside and Dollar study explicitly models the simultaneous interactions among aid, policy, and growth. This approach faces an identification problem of whether aid causes policy or good policy attracts aid. It would appear that there is no simple answer to this identification problem. However, the studies of aid in some recipient countries (e.g., Tanzania) have suggested that it is important to distinguish the practice of the 1960s and 1970s on the one hand from the practice of the 1980s and 1990s on the other. During the 1970s aid allocation was influenced by the degree to which the development philosophy proclaimed by the recipient country was perceived to be congruent to that of the donor. It is in this context that Tanzania, for instance, received considerable aid from social democratic governments of the time. Change of governments in the North in the late 1970s (e.g., United States, United Kingdom, Germany) coincided with questioning these kinds of relationships between aid and policy. At this time questions of macroeconomic policies were introduced in the aid agenda. In the 1980s explicit reference began to be made to the kinds of macroeconomic policies that countries should be pursuing if they were to continue receiving aid from multilateral financial institutions (IMF and World Bank). In response to the perception that aid effectiveness was impaired by pursuit of poor policies, donors—led by the multilateral institutions—became quite explicit in tying aid to the kinds of policies that the recipient countries were pursuing. Even when bilateral donors were not explicit about this new policy stance taken by the multilateral institutions, their actions were influenced it. In this context, the concept of "seal of approval" gained recognition in the literature on aid and policymaking in developing countries.

A further point is that over time there has been policy learning on the part of governments and multilateral institutions that have been administering policy conditionality. What was "good" policy in the mid-1980s has been modified considerably since the 1990s (e.g., the Comprehensive Development Framework). It is clear that the concept of "good" policies has also been evolving, benefiting from experience over time. In this context, to invoke regression analysis using a fixed index of policy over a long period of time can lead to ambiguous results.

Guillaumont and Chauvet have highlighted the influence of external factors on aid effectiveness. In their study, based on cross-sectional econometric tests, they found that aid effectiveness depends on the external and climatic environment to a larger extent than on good domestic policies.[28] They propose the adoption of the principle of performance-based aid allocation whereby performance would be adjusted for the impact of environmental factors. According to such a principle, more aid would be allocated the worse the external environment (for a given policy) and the better the policy (for a given external environment). It is shown that the influence of aid is more positive in countries that are more vulnerable to exogenous factors. The positive influence arises from the role of aid in dampening the negative effects of hostile external factors.[29]

To use such weak results to make strong policy prescriptions like "direct aid only to countries with sound economic management" ignores the reality that countries lacking good policies may need assistance of one type or another to help them get back on track. The world economic environment has changed considerably and the development paradigms and policies that may have worked in the last three decades may not necessarily be the most appropriate in the new century. Using past performance as an indicator of future performance could be dubious in a new world economic environment given the incomplete understanding of the interplay among aid, macro-economic policy, and political economy variables.[30] Therefore the unresolved issue is how and whether the different kinds of aid instruments at hand can be made to work better in varying country circumstances.

NOTES

[1] Increasing amounts of aid are now provided to NGOs. However, the percentage of ODA provided to NGOs remains relatively small—5 percent or less according to the DAC. Our analysis here will not include aid to NGOs or their dependence on that aid, although it is to be hoped that a study of aid dependence on the part of NGOs will be undertaken in the future.

[2] World Bank, *Can Africa Claim the 21st Century?* (Washington, DC: World Bank, 2000). This report is a product of a collaborative initiative of five institutions (World Bank, African Development Bank, African Economic Research Consortium, U.N. Economic Commission for Africa, and the Global Coalition for Africa).

[3] See Carol Lancaster, *Aid to Africa: So Much to Do, So Little Done* (Chicago: University of Chicago Press, 1999).

[4] Julius Nyerere, *Freedom and Socialism* (New York: Oxford University Press, 1968), p. 238.

[5] DAC, *Development Cooperation 1998* (Paris: OECD, 1999), p. A65.

[6] A recent World Bank report identifies 32 SAPS in 17 African countries, including Benin, Burkina Faso, Cameroon, Cote d'Ivoire, Ethiopia, Ghana, Guinea, Kenya, Madagascar, Mali, Mauritania, Mozambique, Niger, Senegal, Tanzania, Uganda, and Zambia. See World Bank, *Tracking of Support Provided under Sector Programs*, Special Program of Action Working Group on Economic Management (Washington, DC: World Bank, April 1999), p.13.

[7] Peter Harrold and Associates, "The Broad Sector Approach to Development Lending," World Bank Discussion Paper No. 302 (Washington, DC: World Bank, 1995), p. xiv.

[8] Oxford Policy Management, *Sector Investment Programmes in Africa: Issues and Experience; Evidence from Case Studies*, Seminar on Sector Investment Programs, SPA Donors' Meeting, Paris, 1996.

[9] World Bank, *Tracking of Support*, op. cit. note 6, p. 6.

[10] Ibrahim Elbadawi, "External Aid: Help or Hindrance to Export Orientation in Africa," in Economic Commission for Africa, *Financing Africa's Development: Issues on Aid Effectiveness*, background paper, Addis Ababa, 1999.

[11] Prepared for the African Economic Research Consortium, Nairobi, Kenya, June 1998, mimeo.

[12] M. T. Hadjimichael et al., "Sub-Saharan Africa: Growth, Savings, and Investment, 1986-93," Occasional Paper No. 118 (Washington, DC: International Monetary Fund, 2000).

[13] Paul Collier, "The Failure of Conditionality," in *Perspectives on Aid and Development*, ed. Catherine Gwin and Joan M. Nelson, Policy Essay No. 22 (Washington, DC: ODC, 1997), p. 54.

[14] Howard White, "Foreign Aid, Taxes, and Public Investment: A Further Comment," *Journal of Development Economics*, 1994.

[15] S. Devarajan, A.S. Rajkumar, and V. Swaroop, "What Does Aid to Africa Finance?" ODC/AERC Project on Managing a Smooth Transition from Aid Dependence in Africa, 1998.

[16] Jean-Paul Azam and Seraphine Fouda, "The Economic Impact of Aid on Recipients," framework paper prepared for ODC/AERC Project on Managing a Smooth Transition from Aid Dependence in Africa, 1998.

[17] This was among the findings of David Dollar and Craig Burnside, *Assessing Aid* (Washington, DC: World Bank,1998). These results were based on a worldwide sample of countries.

[18] See Collier, "The Failure of Conditionality," op. cit. note 13, pp. 8-9.

[19] Robert Lensink and Oliver Morrissey, "Aid Instability as a Measure of Uncertainty and the Positive Impact of Aid on Growth," University of Nottingham, UK, 1999.

[20] See Paul Collier, "Aid Dependency: A Critique," in *Financing Africa's Development: Issues on Aid Effectiveness* (Addis Ababa, Ethiopia: Economic Commission for Africa, May 1999), p. 10.

[21] Much of this section is drawn from Deborah Brautigam and Kwesi Botchwey, "The Institutional Impact of Aid Dependence on Recipients in Africa," framework paper prepared for the ODC/AERC Project on Managing a Smooth Transition from Aid Dependence in Africa, October 1998.

[22] Royal Danish Ministry of Foreign Affairs, *Report of the Group of Independent Advisors of Development Cooperation Issues Between Tanzania and Its Aid Donors*, known as "The Helleiner Report," June 1995.

[23] Professor Helleiner has been invited at least three times to review progress made by both donors and Tanzania on points that were agreed upon in January 1997. He came in December 1997, March 1999, and May 2000, and each time he presented a report of progress made. Note that these reports were internal documents for discussion between the government and the donors and are not available to the public as such.

[24] Marc Wuyts, "Foreign Aid, Structural Adjustment and Public Management: The Mozambiquan Experience," Institute of Strategic Studies Working Paper, General Series No. 206, November 1995.

[25] African governments have long ago learned how to manage relationships with their aid donors to limit the influence of the latter. However, even if they can limit the influence of the pipers who are paying them, aid dependent African governments still have fewer incentives to be accountable to their own populations.

[26] Azam and Fouda, "The Economic Impact of Aid," op. cit. note 16.

[27] Burnside and Dollar, *Assessing Aid*, op. cit. note 17.

[28] Patrick Guillaumont and Lisa Chauvet, *Aid and Performance: A Reassessment* (Clermont-Ferrand, France: CERDI, 1999).

[29] Guillaumont and Chauvet, *Aid and Performance,* op. cit. note 28.

[30] Henrik Hansen and Finn Tarp, "Aid Effectiveness Disputed," in *Foreign Aid and Development,* ed. Finn Tarp (London: Routledge, 1999).

Chapter 3
Strategies for a
Smooth Transition from
Aid Dependence in Africa

This essay began with the question of whether aid dependence in Africa was part of the problem of development or part of the solution. The answer, we find, is that aid dependence in Africa can be either, depending on the policies and institutions of the African governments receiving the aid and those of the donor governments and international organizations providing it.

Reduction of aid dependence is likely to be realized if existing aid is made more effective. When aid is effective, then more of it can be justified in the initial phases in order to build the capacity to manage the economy with less aid. The implication is that aid management needs to change considerably from past practices on the part of recipients and donors alike. The interaction between aid and institutional "learning by doing" by the recipient is important and should be cultivated in a way that promotes institutional capacity building rather than capacity erosion.

Broadly speaking, there are three strategies for managing a smooth transition from aid dependence in Africa, depending on the *capacity* and the *commitment* of African governments to development:

- **Countries with governments that are both capable and committed.** These countries should be able to handle relatively large amounts of aid well. The strategy for reducing their aid dependence would be for aid to rise for a period as needed and then, as less external concessional assistance is required, to taper off. The degree of aid dependence and period of time over which that dependence will increase and then decrease will depend on the needs of the particular country.

- **Countries with governments that lack both capacity and commitment.** Where these countries are aid dependent, donors will want to implement a strategy of gradually reducing that dependence until a government with a strong commitment to development appears.

- **Countries with governments that have limited capacity but a significant commitment to the development of their people.** Here, the broad outlines of a strategy for reducing aid dependence might include an emphasis on strengthening the capacity of the government and civil society organizations and on adjusting the levels of aid and, above all, the management of aid, to amounts the recipient government can handle effectively.

Behind these categories of countries is the concept of "selectivity"— deciding on the level and type of aid according to not just need but also the capacity and commitment of the government of the country. The three separate categories of countries described here require considerable refinement: How do we identify and measure capacity and commitment? (The World Bank reportedly has made a start on this effort by developing measures of institutional capacity in African countries. However, these remain confidential.) It is beyond the scope of this essay to produce such measures, but they would constitute an important first step to implementing a policy of true selectivity on the part of aid donors.[1]

The remainder of this chapter will examine the elements of these strategies for managing a smooth transition from aid dependence in Africa. The strategy of increasing aid dependence to spur development and then decreasing it is exemplified by Botswana. Our discussion of this strategy will center on the experience of that country. (It is not suggested here that the Government of Botswana consciously pursued a strategy for a smooth transition from aid dependence. But its experience demonstrates how such a strategy might work for other countries in Africa.) We shall then examine several common elements in a strategy for a smooth transition from aid dependence in the other two categories of countries.

· ·

CAPABLE AND COMMITTED: BOTSWANA'S TRANSITION FROM AID DEPENDENCE

■ BOTSWANA IS A UNIQUE CASE STUDY OF AID DEPENDENCE in Africa. It has gone from being one of the poorest, most aid dependent countries to a middle-income country no longer in need of significant amounts of external assistance and where aid donors have begun to phase out that assistance. Table 3 charts the evolution of two of the principle indicators of aid dependence in Botswana over two decades.

Other economic indicators show a similar story of high aid dependence in the 1970s and through part of the 1980s and then a rapid decline in the 1990s. We know from available data and literature that at independence in 1966 Botswana was dependent on aid primarily from the

United Kingdom for its entire development budget as well as a portion of other government expenditures.

What has been the impact of the high level of aid dependence on Botswana's institutions and economy? Aid dependence appears to have benefited Botswana's development and avoided the negative consequences for institutions and the economy described in the previous chapter on aid dependence in Africa. Specifically, aid has helped the Government of Botswana finance the technical assistance it desperately needed at the beginning of the independence period and still requires to a much lesser extent today. It has helped the government expand education and health services for the population. And it funded geological explorations and later the infrastructure needed to attract foreign investment in Botswana's rich natural resources, especially diamonds. The investments in diamonds and other minerals have greatly expanded the country's income and the revenues of the Botswana government, which it then used to further expand infrastructure, education, health, and other services that have led to a significant improvement in health, literacy, and life expectancy.[2]

How do we explain the positive contribution of aid and a dependence on aid to Botswana's development? Two major factors account for this positive outcome: 1) Botswana's government managed its *economy* effectively; and 2) it managed its *foreign aid* effectively.

First and most important, the Government of Botswana has been competent, clean, disciplined, and effective in managing its economy. It has been able to plan and implement economic policies and programs effectively for growth. The Botswana government recognized early on that if it was to enjoy rapid growth, it needed to exploit its mineral resources. Its small size, the limited education of its population, and the aridity of its climate constrained its potential as either an agricultural (except for livestock) or industrial producer. Exploiting its mineral resources was the obvious strategy for promoting rapid growth. This strategy proved effective with rising export earnings from diamond production and one of the highest growth rates in the world over an extended period. The government plowed a portion of revenues from diamonds and other mineral exports back into infrastructure and the expansion of health, education, and other services. The rest it invested abroad and used the returns to fund government expenditures. By the mid-1990s, Botswana was no longer a low-income country. Poverty was declining and most of its citizens had access to basic services. (However, there was still large-scale unemployment, and inequalities in incomes were widening.)

The Government of Botswana has been prudent in the use of its windfall profits from mineral exports—something most other African governments have proven incapable of doing. It adopted a policy at independence of "making the country a financially viable entity in the shortest period of time" and has stuck to it.[3] It has worked hard to ensure that government officials are adequately trained to fulfill their responsibilities and has been willing to retain expatriates where Botswanans were not available to fill particular posts. Public officials (and often political leaders) have remained in their jobs for extended periods, giving them the experience to be effective. And it has avoided the patronage-based politics and resource allocations and the corruption that have vitiated the efforts of other African governments to spur their country's growth.

More broadly, governance in Botswana has been effective and the political system stable. Botswana is a democracy, with multiple parties, periodic elections, and a free press. The government utilizes the traditional village *kogotla* to consult with citizens on important policy issues and, in recent years, has held national consultations on development plans. However, Botswana does not have all the characteristics of democracy that Western observers expect. There has never been an alternation—that is, the ruling party has yet to be defeated and replaced by an opposition party. And civil society (so often regarded by Western officials as essential to a functioning democracy) is weak and plays relatively little role in Botswanan political life.[4]

A second major factor in the positive consequences of aid dependence in Botswana is that the government has managed its aid exceptionally effectively. But most important, the government has been organized and capable of integrating aid into its broader development plans and priorities, and it has been willing to reject aid that did not fit those priorities. Specifically, both planning and budgeting have been centralized in the Ministry of Finance and Development. That ministry develops government spending and investment plans for several years into the future and the associated budgets of particular ministries. It then has sought out aid donors to fund projects—usually according to the donor's particular policy orientations. Donors have not been permitted to deal directly with spending ministries in developing aid-funded activities or to create stand-alone organizations to implement their aid projects as they have done in so many other African countries. The government has maintained the integrity and discipline of this planning and budgeting system over several decades of aid dependence, ensuring that aid monies supported its priorities. In managing its aid donors in this way, the Government of Botswana has not had any need (or desire) to participate in donor coordination efforts such as U.N.-organized roundtables or World Bank consultative groups, and none exists for Botswana.

Aid dependence has risen and, subsequently, with Botswana's remarkable growth over several decades, declined. The country is a classic case of how aid should support development and then decline once a reasonable degree of development has been achieved. What was Botswana's path for transitioning from aid dependence?

It is not clear that the Government of Botswana had a conscious strategy or plan. As we have noted, the government had as its primary goal the creation of a financially independent country as quickly as possible. Also important was reducing the pervasive poverty in the country. To achieve this goal, the political leadership recognized that it was necessary first to create a government that had the capacity to manage effectively and second to identify something Botswana could produce and sell abroad that would enable it to finance its own development. Foreign aid played an important role in achieving each of these goals: it helped finance technical assistance and expatriate expertise needed to create a functioning, effective bureaucracy and to educate and train the Botswanans who could take over from expatriates to "localize" the country's administration. (The government did not rush

to appoint Botswanans to government positions, regardless of their qualifi-
cations—avoiding a mistake made in much of the rest of Africa.) And aid
helped fund the geological exploration that led to the identification of potentially rich mineral resources.

To attract the foreign investment that would develop the mineral
resources, the government built the needed infrastructure—again, with the
help of foreign aid. Once the investments were made and the revenues from
mineral exports rising, the Government of Botswana could begin to achieve
its goal of reducing its aid dependence and this is what happened.[5] Aid then
became primarily a source of funding for technical advice and assistance. And
some aid is still provided, both for technical assistance and for activities, like
conservation, particularly favored by the publics in donor countries.[6] The
path for reducing aid dependence in Botswana—at least in retrospect—was
one of putting in place the basic foundations of development (education and
health services and infrastructure), helping government build its capacity,
and helping to identify economic activities that would eventually raise
national income, export earnings, and government revenues on a sustained
basis. These achievements would then permit the country to both finance
its own future development and manage its affairs effectively.

· ·

LOW CAPACITY,
LOW COMMITMENT

■ FOR COUNTRIES WITH WEAK GOVERNMENTAL CAPACITY and a weak
commitment to development, it is clear that large amounts of aid are likely to
be wasted or even become counterproductive by encouraging those governments to avoid needed reforms while building up debt. In this case, aid
donors should collaborate to develop—with the participation of the government, if possible—a plan for reducing overall aid levels and the dependence
on that aid by the government and society. Even in poor economic performers, it is important that significant reductions in aid are made in a manner
that does not further disrupt the economy and society. Where possible, aid
agencies should consider providing modest amounts of assistance for
education and to NGOs providing needed services within the society.
Appropriate forms of capacity building should be designed and supported

with a view to raising the low levels of capacity. In addition, various forms of assistance in the form of development ideas should be given priority to build up understanding and commitment.

LOW CAPACITY, VARYING COMMITMENT

■ THE NUMBER OF COUNTRIES FALLING INTO THE low commitment/low capacity category is likely to be small at present (apart from those involved in civil conflict). Many more countries share the problems of weak capacity combined with commitments of varying degrees to development.

One important element in this strategy for this third category of countries is a concerted effort on the part of both donors and African officials to strengthen the capacity of governments to manage their resources, including aid resources, effectively. The elements in such a strategy are well recognized:

■ adequately trained staff, competent leadership, and effective organization;

■ strong analytical capacities;

■ an effective planning function (including reliable data);

■ a disciplined and transparent budgetary process involving the entire government;

■ a capability to implement, evaluate, and learn from past efforts; and

■ a strong auditing function.

Behind these systems and processes are hiring, promoting, and firing policies based on merit rather than political contacts. And basic to an effective capacity in government is the rule of law. Corruption, whether for political or personal gain, can corrode capacity in the best of organizations.

A strategy for managing a smooth transition from aid dependence will vary significantly from country to country, depending on its needs, capacity, and commitment. In some countries, it may make sense to plan for immediate increases in aid (where capacity can be quickly strengthened), followed by a decrease in aid dependence in the future. In some countries, the emphasis in the near term will be on improving capacity. The requirements of aid largely for capacity building will need to be established on a case-by-case basis depending on the capacity-building strategy adopted.

For all three of the above categories, we do not propose to offer a detailed template for such strategies. But for most countries falling into this broad category, a strategy for a smooth transition from aid dependence will have three key elements: addressing the problem of debt; developing a plan on the part both of aid donors and the recipient government to manage a smooth and responsible transition from aid dependence; and improving the modalities of aid delivery on the part of the donors of that aid. Most of these countries will also have unfinished economic reform agendas that need to be completed as well.

. . . .

DEBT

■   THE BURDEN OF DEBT REMAINS A HEAVY ONE in much of Sub-Saharan Africa. This debt is primarily owed to governments and international organizations rather than to private creditors. One-third is owed to multilateral lenders such as the World Bank; another 44 percent is owed to governments. In Africa's poorer countries, these proportions are higher, with private debt correspondingly smaller.[7]

We have seen from the framework paper by Devarajan and his colleagues and from a number of the studies on which this essay is based that African governments typically use a portion of their aid inflows to service their debts. If there is to be a smooth transition from aid dependence in any African country, the burden of debt servicing must also be reduced. That would reduce the transaction costs to African governments of managing that aid. For those where a reduction in aid levels and aid dependence is contemplated, debt reduction will be absolutely essential. Decreases in aid in the absence of a reduction in debt servicing would make the drain on government resources represented by debt repayments proportionately greater and resources available for development purposes correspondingly fewer (assuming that those governments would even continue to service their debts).

The HIPC Initiative, proposed by the World Bank in 1998 and since liberalized, is the first international response that provides comprehensive debt relief to the world's poorest, most heavily indebted countries by removing the debt overhang for countries that pursue economic and social reforms targeted at measurable poverty reduction. In addition, it helps countries exit from endless debt restructuring to lasting debt relief and it reduces multilateral debt. It goes some way toward reducing the burden of debt in qualifying countries in Africa and elsewhere, but the procedure for qualifying remains complicated and time consuming.

The HIPC Initiative was enhanced by late 1998, first with a view to deepen and broaden debt relief by cutting external debt servicing by more than $50 billion—more than twice the relief provided under the original HIPC. When completed in combination with traditional debt relief, the initiative will cut by more than one-half the outstanding debt of more than 30 countries. The World Bank itself will reduce its debt claims by some $12 billion. Second, the changes to HIPC will allow the World Bank and the IMF (in a similar approach) to provide immediate debt relief at the point that HIPC assistance is approved. And, third, the initiative aims to strongly link debt relief and poverty reduction by freeing up resources, which will be used to support poverty reduction strategies developed with civil society.

The World Bank and the IMF have worked proactively toward rapid implementation of the initiative: 14 countries have qualified, at least preliminarily, for debt relief packages amounting to approximately $23 billion, of which nine have formally qualified for more than $14 billion in debt relief and five have qualified preliminarily for an additional $9 billion. With continued progress in economic and social reforms programs, debt relief packages for up to 20 countries was expected to be in place by the end of 2000.

If aid agencies and African governments are to collaborate successfully in a plan for reducing aid dependence in the region, a reduction in the burden of debt servicing must be part of that strategy. The latest developments in the HIPC Initiative have linked debt relief to poverty reduction. This has been meant that potential beneficiaries would qualify for debt relief if they prepare acceptable policy documents known as Poverty Reduction Strategy Papers. It further requires the preparation of these strategy papers to be participatory. The conditions are meant to improve the quality of poverty reducing policymaking and enhance governance. This is a positive development, but it is too early to evaluate comprehensively the effectiveness of this broadened and deepened HIPC Initiative.

A TRANSITION PLAN

■   ANOTHER CRITICAL ELEMENT IN A STRATEGY for reducing aid dependence is a plan on the part of the recipient government—negotiated with donors and announced publicly—that reduces overall aid flows and aid dependence over an agreed period (even if for some countries it may be necessary to increase aid levels in the initial years). The plan should also combine expenditure reductions, increased taxes, maintenance of key social services, efforts to mobilize additional savings and domestic and foreign investment, and promoting export earnings to replace, in so far as possible, aid flows.

To achieve increased levels and efficiency of private investments, recipient countries must address a number of policy constraints and undertake strategic initiatives. Sustained private investments require a stable macroeconomic environment and a significant improvement in the overall quality of governance, specifically, physical security, the observance of basic human rights, the rule of law, and accountability and transparency in public and private transactions. Furthermore, policy recommendations to strengthen private investments can only be made with a clear understanding of the constraints affecting private investments. One mechanism of ensuring continuous understanding and follow-up on private investors' constraints could be the establishment of private sector consultative arrangements.[8]

The challenge for export promotion is to increase the volume, diversity, and value of the country's exports of goods and services. Its promotion will help to close the foreign exchange gap currently being met by foreign aid. This can only be matched by a credible government action and capacity for action within both the public and private sectors. Priority should be on building the capacity to supply on a competitive basis.

Export diversification should also receive great attention and is vital for two reasons. First, export receipts have been limited by lost trade shares for traditional products and by concentration on a few primary commodities with low demand elasticity. The prices of these staples, though volatile, are expected to continue their long-run decline. Second, given Africa's small economies, it is hard to imagine a successful diversification drive based solely on domestic markets. For the same reason, exports—especially of industrial and nontraditional products—provide the best avenue for attracting high and productive investment. It bears noting that without broad and growing markets, investment will not be attracted to Sub-Saharan Africa or all of Africa for that matter. Sub-Saharan Africa can diversify and be competitive across a broad range of products, if policies are improved and transaction costs are lowered.

Improvement in infrastructure requires a strategy that will attract private investment and will address the most pressing infrastructure constraints such as poor quality and limited availability.

A private-sector-led strategy for reducing aid dependence requires a stable and dynamic financial sector. Ideally, the financial sector should enable viable businesses to have access to loan and equity finance on affordable terms. A credible strategy for strengthening the financial sector is to strengthen local banks and to promote greater competition within the banking sector. In addition, efforts must be made to provide equity finance to small- and medium-sized companies and to foster institutions.

Development of human capital calls for essential improvements in public health, an effective management of population growth, and increased access to quality education.

This plan, which may include an increase in aid before aid dependence is reduced, could be built on the Comprehensive Development Framework (CDF), proposed by the World Bank and now being elaborated in a number of developing countries. Country-focused CDF's could be extended to include such a strategy on the part of African governments in consultation with their own peoples as well as aid donors, which could also be useful in educating all parties to the aid and development realities in particular countries as well as building national consensus on such a strategy.

. . . .

THE MANAGEMENT OF FOREIGN AID IN A TRANSITION FROM AID DEPENDENCE

■   ONE OF THE PRINCIPAL FINDINGS OF THIS ESSAY is that institutions matter when it comes to the impact of aid dependence as well as other aspects of development. One side of the problem of institutions is the African side—involving the capacity and competence of African governments. The other side is that of the donors. There is evidence that the way aid agencies have managed their assistance in Africa in a number of our case studies has weakened rather than strengthened recipient governments. Part of a strategy for managing a smooth transition from aid dependence involves the donors of that aid and must include a completion of the existing reform agenda involving selectivity, participation, and elaboration and implementation of new modalities.

An effective policy of selectivity must involve two things: a reasonably objective way of measuring the quality of policies and institutions of African governments, and a willingness on the part of aid donors to collaborate in implementing such a policy. We do not yet have the way to measure, and aid donors, often following their political or commercial interests, appear far from being prepared to collaborate effectively in the allocation of aid by country. Until they do, a policy of selectivity will lack credibility.

Policies of participation and partnership also have their limits. Both imply that aid agencies will have to cede some influence over their programs to other organizations if the views of their partners are to be taken seriously. This will be a political challenge to some aid agencies—especially those whose decisions are highly constrained by their own domestic politics. It will also be a challenge to the culture and past patterns of decision making for aid agencies accustomed to controlling how their aid is used in Africa. A recent World Bank evaluation of aid coordination summarized the current situation in the following observation: "Policies of the Bank . . . and of the broader development community . . . have not succeeded in putting the [recipient] country in the driver's seat."[9]

A similar challenge to aid donors of coordination and discipline attaches to the SIPs. At this point, not all aid donors are able or willing to participate in these arrangements. The United States, France, and others, for example, remain outside these efforts. The fact remains that the larger the number of major donors not participating, the smaller the impact of SIPs on the well-recognized problems of aid management in Africa.

There is need to monitor the transition by donors toward transparency and provision of critical information. This is one important step toward improving donor practices as suggested by Helleiner.[10] Aid donors should comply with recipients' governmental requests for information on their current and past activities and their intentions. Some donors may readily be able to supply some information but not all. Standardized and timely aid data should therefore be an important performance indicator for donors. Donor-recipient dialogue should be able to engender agreement as to what is most useful and feasible to supply. A second step in improving donor practices is improving integration and coordination within national plans and priorities so as to prevent donors from imposing their own agendas, as they have often done in the past, and "pushing" projects that are not high in the recipients' priorities. Third, for effective policymaking, one must have reasonably accurate resource projections on a year-by-year basis and preferably for longer periods: enhanced predictability and reliability of resources inflows is required. Last, the tying of aid needs to be reduced, because it has long been recognized as costly to recipients, particularly when it relates both to its use and to its procurement source.

These are some of the important problems still to be addressed by aid donors in improving the management of their aid in Africa. The resolution of these problems remains an essential part of a strategy for managing a smooth transition from aid dependence in the region.

. . . .

NON-AID APPROACHES FOR REDUCING AID DEPENDENCE IN AFRICA

■   IDEALLY, AID DEPENDENCE SHOULD FALL as African economies grow and prosper. To achieve healthy and sustained growth, these economies need not only to get their policies right and strengthen their institutions, but they need investment and foreign markets in which to sell their products. There is no reason why African countries cannot follow Asian countries into light manufacturing as a start on a more rapid growth path. (It is assumed that these countries will continue to expand their export of primary products as well.) An easing in access to the markets of developed countries to sell such commodities as apparel and shoes could be exceedingly helpful by stimulating investment and, more broadly, by focusing the attention of potential international capital on opportunities in African markets. The African Growth and Opportunity Act in the United States and the new Lomé Agreement in Europe offer such market-opening opportunities. These mark a good start in assisting African governments committed to development to attract investment and to expand jobs, exports, national income, and growth. Other developed countries, such as Japan, should consider similar policies to encourage investment and growth in the region—essential in the long run to a transition from aid dependence and healthy growth.

In the end, only Africans can develop Africa. Foreign aid was always intended to help them help themselves. Because economic progress has been limited for so long in so many countries, foreign aid has become for many a source of dependence. The challenge before both the donor community and Africans themselves is to develop and implement effective strategies that will lead to a reduction in that dependence. This essay is an effort to contribute to the discourse that will help both groups move in that direction.

NOTES

[1] Most aid agencies—bilateral and multilateral—already subscribe to a policy of selectivity. But for most donors, the policy remains vague and loosely applied.

[2] Unfortunately, the gains in life expectancy from 45 years at independence to 65 years in the 1990s are now being lost as a result of the impact of HIV/AIDS which, it is estimated, has infected one-quarter of the population. Life expectancy is now projected to decline to 50 or below in the coming years. See Gervase Maipose and Gloria Somolekae, "Managing the Transition from Aid Dependency: The Case of Botswana," case study prepared for the ODC/AERC Project on Managing a Smooth Transition from Aid Dependence in Africa, 1999, p. 46.

[3] Maipose and Somolekae, "The Case of Botswana," op. cit. note 2, p. 8.

[4] Maipose and Somolekae, "The Case of Botswana," op. cit. note 2.

[5] It appears that aid donors took the first step in reducing aid levels as they shifted their resources to poorer countries. Some Botswanan officials complained that their country was being "punished" for its economic success—implying that foreign aid should continue at high levels. However, it appears that most Botswanans recognize that foreign aid has functioned effectively, thereby reducing the need for it.

[6] Not all aid-funded activities in Botswana were equally successful. Efforts to promote agricultural development were not very effective, partly as a result of the aridity of the country and the difficult physical environment there.

[7] World Bank, *Global Development Finance, Analysis and Summary Tables* (Washington, DC: World Bank, 1999,) p. 201.

[8] For more on private investment in Africa, see Vijaya Ramachandran, *Investing in Africa*, Policy Essay No. 29 (Washington, DC: ODC, forthcoming October 2000).

[9] World Bank, Operations Evaluation Department, *The Drive to Partnership: Aid Coordination and the World Bank* (Washington, DC: World Bank, 1999), summarized in World Bank, *OED Reach: Aid Coordination* (Washington, DC: World Bank, November 1999), p. 1.

[10] Gerry Helleiner, "Tanzania Assistance Strategy: Critical Issues," paper prepared for the Tanzania Consultative Group and Related Meetings, Dar es Salaam, Tanzania, May 22-26, 2000.

About the Authors

CAROL LANCASTER is an Associate Professor and Director of the Masters of Science in Foreign Service at Georgetown University. She has served in a number of posts in government, including as Deputy Administrator of USAID (1993-96) and Deputy Assistant Secretary of State for Africa (1980-81). She has also written extensively on foreign aid, foreign policy, and development in Africa. Her latest books include *Aid to Africa* (Chicago University Press, 1999) and *Transforming Foreign Aid* (Institute for International Economics, 2000).

SAMUEL WANGWE is the Executive Director of the Economic and Social Research Foundation, which is a nonprofit policy research NGO based in Dar es Salaam, Tanzania. He has worked in the Economics Department at the University of Dar es Salaam from 1972 where he rose to full professor in 1985 and was head of Economics Department and Dean of the Faculty of Arts and Social Sciences. Before taking up his current position, he worked at the United Nations University's Institute for New Technologies as a senior research fellow from 1991 to 1994. Professor Wangwe has vast experience accumulated over 25 years in academia, research, and consultancy work with both local and international institutions in the areas of economic management, management of aid, industrialization-, trade- and technology-related issues, structural adjustment and the reform process and capacity building. He has authored numerous articles and books including *Exporting Africa: Technology, Trade and Industrialisation in Sub-Saharan Africa*. He has also undertaken extensive policy advisory work for the Government of Tanzania and international organizations.

About the Project

A E R C / O D C COLLABORATIVE PROJECT
ON MANAGING A SMOOTH TRANSITION
FROM AID DEPENDENCE IN AFRICA

The Project on Managing a Smooth Transition from Aid Dependence in Africa, a collaboration of the African Economic Research Consortium (Nairobi) and the Overseas Development Council (Washington), assesses the nature of the problem of aid dependence in Africa and proposes to African countries and their donors strategies for managing effective transitions from todayís high aid dependence situations. Its aim is to both improve understanding of the impact of aid dependence and provide guidance to policymakers, in Africa and abroad, on how to manage a reduction of that dependence so as to enhance, rather than disrupt, economic and political progress in the region and speed up African countries' integration into the world economy.

The project has three components. The first is a set of framework papers that address the basic questions of what aid dependence is, what its impact has been, and how to reduce it constructively. These papers provide guidance for the second component, which is a series of eight country case studies on the impact of aid dependence and how to reduce it in specific contexts. The third component—namely, this Policy Essay—entails the publication and dissemination of the project findings to the research and policy communities in African and donor countries and the international aid institutions.

The project is jointly managed by the AERC and the ODC. These two institutions share responsibility for the project's design and co-manage its implementation. The project is coordinated by Samuel Wangwe, Director of the Economic and Social Research Foundation in Dar es Salaam, Tanzania, and Carol Lancaster, ODC Visiting Fellow and Georgetown University School of Foreign Service Professor. AERC and ODC appointed a small steering committee to advise on substantive elements of the project and to ensure the intellectual quality and policy relevance of the project outputs. The steering committee is co-chaired by the AERC Research Director Augustin Fosu (and earlier by Ibrahim Elbadawi) and ODC Senior Vice President Catherine Gwin. Steering committee members are experts drawn from the research and policy communities in African and donor countries.

The project is funded by multiple donors, which include: the Swedish International Development Cooperation Agency, the U.S. Agency for International Development, the Department for International Development of the United Kingdom, the Swiss Agency for Development and Cooperation, and the Government of Japan.

Project Steering Committee

A E R C / O D C C O L L A B O R A T I V E P R O J E C T
O N M A N A G I N G A S M O O T H T R A N S I T I O N
F R O M A I D D E P E N D E N C E I N A F R I C A

CO-CHAIRS

AUGUSTIN FOSU[a]
AERC Director of Research
Kenya

CATHERINE GWIN
ODC Senior Vice President
United States

**PROJECT
DIRECTORS**

CAROL LANCASTER
ODC/Georgetown University
United States

SAMUEL WANGWE
Economic and Social
 Research Foundation
Tanzania

MEMBERS

ALI ALI
UNECA
Ethiopia

JEAN-PAUL AZAM
Université des Sciences Sociales
France

ROBERT BATES
Harvard University
United States

JEAN BOSSUYT
ECDPM
The Netherlands

PAUL COLLIER
World Bank
United States

ALAN GELB
World Bank
United States

WILLIAM KALEMA
Uganda

RAVI KANBUR
Cornell University
United States

HIROHISA KOHAMA
University of Shizuoka
Japan

DELPHIN RWEGASIRA[b]
AERC Executive Director
Kenya

GERMINA SSEMOGERERE
Makerere University
Uganda

KERFALLA YANSANE
Guinea

[a] Ibrahim Elbadawi served on the committee before his term as AERC of Research Director expired.
[b] Benno Ndulu served on the committee before his term as AERC Executive Director expired.

Note: Affiliations for identification only.

About the ODC

The Overseas Development Council (ODC) is an independent, international policy research institution based in Washington, DC, that seeks to improve decision making on multilateral cooperation in order to promote more effective development and the better management of related global problems. Its program focuses on the interrelationship of globalization and development, and improved multilateral responses to these linked challenges.

To this end, ODC provides analysis, information, and evaluation of multilateral policies, actions, and institutions; develops innovative ideas and new policy proposals; and creates opportunities for decision makers and other interested parties to participate in discussions of critical global issues and decisions.

ODC is governed by an international Board of Directors of recognized and widely respected policy leaders on multilateral development and global issues. Peter D. Sutherland is its Chairman, and John W. Sewell is ODC's President.

ODC is a private, nonprofit organization, funded by foundations, governments, and private individuals.

O | D | C

OVERSEAS DEVELOPMENT COUNCIL
1875 CONNECTICUT AVENUE, NW
SUITE 1012
WASHINGTON, DC 20009
TEL. 202-234-8701
FAX 202-745-0067
http://www.odc.org

POLICY ESSAY NO. 28

About the AERC

The African Economic Research Consortium (AERC), established in 1988, is a public not-for-profit organization devoted to advanced policy research and training. The principal objective is to strengthen local capacity for conducting independent, rigorous inquiry into problems pertinent to the management of economies in Sub-Saharan Africa.

In response to special needs of the region, the AERC Research Program has adopted a flexible approach to improve the technical skills of local researchers, allow for regional determination of research priorities, strengthen national institutions concerned with economic policy research, and facilitate closer ties between researchers and policy makers. The Training Program augments the pool of economic researchers in Sub-Saharan Africa by supporting graduate studies in economics as well as improving the capacities of departments of economics in local public universities. AERC is supported by donor governments, private foundations and international organizations.

AFRICAN ECONOMIC RESEARCH CONSORTIUM
INTERNATIONAL HOUSE, 8TH FLOOR
P.O. BOX 62882
NAIROBI, KENYA

OVERSEAS DEVELOPMENT COUNCIL

**ECONOMIC DEVELOPMENT
POLICY ESSAY NO.28**

Managing a Smooth Transition from Aid Dependence in Africa

Carol Lancaster and Samuel Wangwe

· ·

Many countries in Sub-Saharan Africa are among the poorest in the world with the largest proportions of their populations in poverty and the lowest indicators of social progress. Many of these same countries are also among the most aid dependent in the world. And yet there is evidence that aid in large quantities is a double-edged sword; large amounts of aid over an extended period of time can make the strong stronger and the weak weaker. What, then, is to be done about aid dependence in Africa?

In this essay, the culmination of a two-year collaborative study between ODC and the African Economic Research Consortium in Nairobi, the authors explore strategies for reducing aid and aid dependence in Sub-Saharan Africa. They propose a value-free definition of aid dependence, explore in detail the elements and impact dependence (especially on recipient institutions and organizations), develop empirical materials on aid dependence in individual African countries, and finally, propose specific strategies for reducing aid dependence.

With the prospect of further decreases in aid to Africa and the rising concerns about the disappointing impact of large flows of aid to many African countries, it is timely and even urgent that the issue of reducing aid dependence be addressed. This essay makes an important contribution toward advancing this important task.

ISBN 1-56517-032-6

90000

56 191FSU PS1 **674]**
05/01 24-950-00 GBC

ISBN: 1-56517-032-6